SOUNDS
GOOD ON
PAPER

SOUNDS GOOD ON PAPER

HOW TO BRING BUSINESS LANGUAGE TO LIFE

Roger Horberry

A & C Black • London

First published in Great Britain 2010

A & C Black Publishers Ltd
36 Soho Square, London W1D 3QY
www.acblack.com

A CIP record for this book is available from the British Library.

ISBN: 9–781–4081–2231–0

This book is produced using paper that is made from wood grown in
managed, sustainable forests. It is natural, renewable and recyclable.
The logging and manufacturing processes conform to the environmental
regulations of the country of origin.

Design by Fiona Pike, Pike Design, Winchester
Typeset by Saxon Graphics, Derby
Printed in the United Kingdom by Cox & Wyman, Reading RG1 8EX

CONTENTS

ABOUT THE AUTHOR

I'm Roger Horberry, I'm 45 and I live in North Yorkshire, a convenient location for my day job as a freelance copywriter working for various London design and branding agencies. Over the last 25 years, I've released a dozen CDs of wilfully obscure music that have quite rightly been ignored by the listening public. I have written one other book — *Brilliant Copywriting: How to Craft the Most Effective Copy Imaginable* (Pearson, 2009). Get in touch at roger@rogerhorberry.com.

ACKNOWLEDGEMENTS

A great big thank you to:

Lucy, Lotte and George; Lindsay and David; Andrew, Alex and Eva; Mark Gravil; John Simmons; the lovely people at www.26.org.uk; and last but not least, Lisa Carden for being the editor from heaven.

The man is most original who can adapt from the greatest number of sources.
Thomas Carlyle 1795-1881

INTRODUCTION

Yoda, the diminutive Jedi Master from *Star Wars*, had a real way with words. Take this typical example of Yoda-speak: 'Fear leads to anger. Anger leads to hate. Hate leads to suffering'. Lovely stuff. It's got a sort of music to it that amplifies its meaning. He could have simply said, 'fear has a number of unpleasant consequences', but Yoda's version has infinitely more eloquence.

Or consider Mike Tyson's reply of, 'I think I'll fade into Bolivian', when asked about his long-term future. OK, he could have been talking about a planned retirement in that beautiful but troubled South American country, but it seems more likely Iron Mike made a mistake. Not just any old error though, this blunder somehow works, albeit in its own illogical way.

Then there's Mark Twain's immortal, 'Reports of my death have been greatly exaggerated'. It's a famously snappy phrase, but from where exactly does it get its snap? It makes sense, then again it doesn't, then again it does...

Something interesting is going on, something deep within language that makes these sentences mean more than the sum of their words. All three are, as if you hadn't guessed, figures of speech – creative turns of phrase that give our words more colour, emphasis and impact. Figures of speech use words in an expressive, non-literal way in order to create a particular effect. In doing so they spice up the meagre fayre of literal language – they are truly the salt, pepper, vinegar and mustard of speech. Without figures we'd be stuck with the stodge of standard-issue words, a distinctly unpalatable prospect.

Once you start looking it becomes clear that figures of speech are all around us. Our everyday language is liberally strewn with phrases and verbal constructions that break the rules of syntax but make sense all the same. In fact despite their incongruity they make *more* sense than straight talk – that's their point. By mining the rich seam of ambiguity that lies between what someone actually says and what we understand their words to mean, figures of speech bring language to life and offer a glimpse into a new world – obscure yet obvious, complex yet commonplace, foreign yet familiar.

WHY FIGURES MATTER

So far, so good, but this book is aimed at anyone who writes as part of their job: what on earth have figures of speech got to do with business writers and words at work? The answer is agreeably simple: figures are a proven way of persuading colleagues and customers to see things our way and getting them to respond accordingly. They provide an arsenal of ready-made wit so you'll never be at a loss for words in tense power meetings. They're a short cut to argumentative excellence, a treasury of pithy one-liners, and a tried and tested way of structuring your thinking for maximum effect.

In short, figures have much to offer the business writer from a practical point of view. They're also great fun and incredibly interesting. And in case you're thinking that 'fun', 'interesting' and 'work' don't go together then I'm here to argue otherwise, at least in the context of language. Business writers who try to bludgeon their readers into submission through a toxic mix of boredom and wordiness rarely succeed. As advertising legend David Ogilvy put it, 'You can't bore someone into reading your ad'. You can, however, interest them into doing so. The same logic applies to emails, web pages, blog entries, reports, case studies, pack copy, scripts, letters, internal comms, brochures, mailers and a hundred other forms of business communication. Although you wouldn't know it from the dross that many companies place in front of their long-suffering customers and employees, *people read and*

Incidentally...

Over 100 years ago James De Mille, Canadian novelist and professor of rhetoric, offered three good reasons for studying figures of speech. Firstly they embellish our writing in a way that makes reading itself more enjoyable. Secondly figures add to our powers of persuasion by refreshing old ideas and suggesting new ones. Thirdly they throw fresh light upon a subject by presenting it in a novel and unexpected way. All useful stuff for anyone who works with words.

remember what interests them, so if you want your words to achieve their purpose then it pays to make them as appealing as possible. And one elegant, effective and highly pleasurable way to do that is through the liberal use of figures of speech.

In Classical times, figures were thought to have almost mystical properties as they displayed a convincing power out of all proportion to the words they used. That's a lovely idea but sadly it's a load of nonsense. What many figures actually do is add a subtle emotional resonance to an otherwise rational argument. If you're trying to persuade someone, then facts are a great start but they're rarely enough on their own. If they were, then datasheets would make effective adverts, and clearly they don't. Instead, what you need is some sort of emotional magic that beguiles your audience into wanting whatever it is you're offering (Aristotle called this appeal to emotion *pathos*). My point is that many buying decisions are made by the heart and not the head. No form of communication is better suited to this process of subtle seduction than our friends the figures of speech. *That's* what figures can do for you and *that's* why everyone who writes as part of their job would do well to acquaint themselves with what follows.

NAMING NAMES

Given their Classical roots, it's no surprise that many figures of speech boast impressively Latinate names. In the Yoda quote we've just seen the figure is an *anadiplosis* (defined as repeating a word or phrase from the end of a sentence or clause at the beginning of the *next* sentence or clause), in Tyson's case it's the more familiar *malapropism* (using a similar sounding but incorrect word) and in Twain's case it's a *meiosis* (intentionally implying that something is of less significance than it really is).

Incidentally...

Compare Yoda's anadiplosis with these lines from Act five, Scene one of Shakespeare's Richard II: 'The love of wicked men converts to fear, That fear to hate, and hate turns one or both, To worthy danger and deserved death.' Are they by any chance related?

Don't be distracted by these names and their somewhat convoluted definitions. What matters is the persuasive power that figures of speech provide, not ploughing through the small print of their descriptions. In fact the definitions and examples associated with a particular figure vary wildly between sources, so much so that it's often hard to know whether two authors are talking about the same figure. And it's not just me who's mystified. No lesser authority than Quintillion, ace Roman orator and expert on all things eloquent observed, 'Writers have given special names to all the figures, but variously and as it pleased them.' Fast-forward around fifteen hundred years and Erasmus of Rotterdam noted that when it comes to rhetorical figures, 'Every definition is a misfortune.' And by the 17th century the poet Samuel Butler was complaining, 'All the rhetorician's rules, teach but the naming of his tools'. My advice is simple: take what you need, enjoy them for what they are, and don't worry too much about the formal side of figures.

DIGGIN' *THE GARDEN OF ELOQUENCE*

No discussion of figure of speech would be complete without a tip o' the hat to *The Garden of Eloquence*. Written by English curate Henry Peacham in 1577, *The Garden of Eloquence* is a treatise on rhetoric that described 184 figures of speech. They range from the familiar to the downright obscure, but the chances are you've probably used a good few of them already today (unless you happen to be reading this during a silent monastic retreat).

The Rev Peacham defined a figure of speech thus:

'… a forme of words, oration, or sentence, made new by arts differing from the vulgar manner and custome of writing or speaking.'

And:

'As stars to give light'

And even more concisely as:

'Wisdom speaking eloquently.'

Delightful. As I say, a surprising number of the figures Henry covered are still in everyday use. For example, he describes a figure of speech called an *eroteme* as, 'to affirm or deny a point by asking it as a question'. That might seem murky until you realise that, 'Why are you so stupid?' is 100 per cent eroteme, as is Homer Simpson's immortal, 'Beer. Is there anything it can't do?'

Then there's Henry's *epitrope*, a figure of speech in which, 'One turns things over to one's hearers, either pathetically, ironically, or in such a way as to suggest a proof of something without having to state it', often in the form of granting permission. Tricky, until you realise that, 'Go ahead punk, make my day', fits the bill perfectly. Despite their age, Henry's figures of speech are clearly alive and well.

LET'S GET ORGANISED

With so many figures to consider, some sort of categorisation seems in order. Classical commentators divided figures of speech into two broad groups – *schemes* (a deviation from the ordinary or expected flow of words, for example a metaphor or simile) and *tropes* (a modification of the usual meaning of a word or phrase, for example a pun or oxymoron).

This two-way split is a well established but highly unhelpful division – neither category name gives any real indication of where a particular figure belongs or what each group actually does. As this book focuses on how figures of speech can help you express yourself at work, it seems appropriate to come up with some rather more practical categories. So in the remainder of this book I've grouped figures by role, with each chapter looking at a common business communication challenge and how a select group of figures can help you rise to it. Here's what's in store:

CHAPTER ONE

Making the mundane marvellous – figures that describe, compare and contrast

Simile, metaphor and **kenning**, also hypocatastasis, antonomasia, enargia, allegory and analogy.

CHAPTER TWO
Drawing attention to yourself – figures that exaggerate, emphasise and illuminate
Tmesis, hyperbole and **pleonasm**, also asterismos, periphrasis, congeries, prolixity, logorrhoea, parenthesis and digression.

CHAPTER THREE
Saying it another way – figures that swap, shift or flip
Metonymy and **euphemism**, also onomatopoeia, synechdoche, amphibology and periphrasis.

CHAPTER FOUR
Turning heads – figures that make the ordinary extraordinary
Chiasmus and **antimetabole**, also hyperbaton, antithesis, anadiplosis and parallelism.

CHAPTER FIVE
Tickling your reader's fancy – figures of fun
Pun and **Zeugma**, also spoonerisms and malapropisms.

CHAPTER SIX
Sounding smart – figures that entertain your ears
Alliteration and **anaphora**, also assonance, dissonance, euphony and resonance.

CHAPTER SEVEN
Words that can wound – figures to provoke, mock or confuse
Oxymoron, irony and **sarcasm**.

CHAPTER EIGHT
Bringing it all together – how rhetoric can rock the business writer's world

USING FIGURES IN REAL LIFE

This book includes many examples of figures in action. Relatively few come from the world of business, and that's why I decided to write this book in the first place. Business language tends to be either self-consciously plain or unnecessarily verbose; rarely is it sparkling, clear and imaginative. There's no reason it shouldn't be all these things, so this book is a quiet plea for everyone who writes as part of their job to bring a touch more creativity to the task.

And while we're on the subject, let's get one thing clear – taking an interest in language is perfectly compatible with hard-nosed commercial concerns like efficiency and results. If a piece of business prose is terminally turgid then the chances are it'll be ignored, in which case it can't possibly achieve its purpose. Whatever time and resources went into creating it will be wasted, a situation that sooner or later costs real money. If using a figure of speech turns a piece of writing into something that your audience reads and enjoys, then there's every chance it'll perform as intended and become an asset rather than a liability. In this modest way, figures of speech can make a real contribution to a business's bottom line.

Don't take my word for it – let's have some real life examples of how figures can animate everyday business communications. We'll start with a familiar figure, the *metaphor*. Taking a metaphor's meaning literally and responding accordingly is a great way of generating snappy comebacks on the fly:

Them: We'll pick the low hanging fruit.
You: Just make sure they're not rotten.

Or:

Them: Just my two-penneth worth.
You: Are you sure it's worth that?

This approach has the added benefit of highlighting just how lazy the original speaker's cliché really is.

A *chiasmus* – the 'reversible raincoat' figure behind John F. Kennedy's famous, 'Ask not what your country can do for you' quote – presents a mirror image of a concept for the purposes of persuasion. It rebuts a point by turning it around. Along the way it can make the commonplace seem compelling:

Them: He's complaining our departmental budget is too big this year.
You: It's not a question of whether we deserve what we get. It's whether we get what we deserve.

Or more succinctly:

Them: Our customers never call us.
You: Do we ever call our customers?

Following on from the stately chiasmus let's look at the *climax*. This figure employs a number of clauses, with the last part of one forming the start of the next. It's great for bringing your argument to a, well, climax. For example, I could promote this book to business people by chaining together a series of climaxing clauses thus:

'Including figures of speech in your writing helps creates interest. Interest means people will remember the message. Remembering the message is the first step towards making a sale. And selling is what this business is all about.'

Next, the *dialysis*, a figure that contrasts two ideas against each other. For example an irate employee might legitimately ask the boss, 'Why do you listen to your mates in the pub but not your own people?' It also comes in a rather nifty no/yes form:

Them: You seemed a little irritable in that meeting.
You: Irritable, no. Infuriated, yes.

This no/yes form is great for redefining an issue and introducing instant wit:

Them: She's his new assistant.
You: New, yes. Of assistance, no.

Finally, see how the *antithesis* weighs one thing against another to make its point with elegance and economy:

'On one hand we could carry on investing and risk losing everything, and on the other we could pull out and fall behind our rivals.'

Notice how the antithesis uses repetition and a parallel structure to create equivalence and clarity in what could otherwise be a complex argument:

'Our competitor pushed up the price of their product but lost half their customers. We kept our price the same and doubled our market share.'

As you can see, figures really do have real life business applications.

I've included these and many other examples throughout this book in an effort to inspire, illustrate, amuse and enthuse. Their aim is to sensitise your subconscious so that given the right circumstances a well-formed figure of speech will spring spontaneously from your lips/pen/fingers/whatever. I suggest that you read, enjoy, and then gently forget, allowing your subconscious to do the rest. Sow the seeds of eloquence and who knows what marvellous blooms will ultimately issue forth?

And on that optimistic note, let's go to work.

CHAPTER ONE

MAKING THE MUNDANE MARVELLOUS

FIGURES THAT DESCRIBE, COMPARE AND CONTRAST

There's a whole family of figures whose sole job is to create the most striking mental images imaginable. What's so impressive about these figures is their ability to pack a mass of meaning into a minute space, which makes them useful tools in the world of business writing where word counts are often restricted. We'll take a good look at *simile*, *metaphor* and *kenning*, followed by a quick peek at *hypocatastasis*, *antonomasia*, *enargia*, *allegory* and *analogy* amongst others. You're probably familiar with simile and metaphor from school, but unless you're a student of Old Norse you may be ignorant of the kenning's considerable charms.

SIMILE
IMAGERY IS EVERYTHING

This friendly little figure works by comparing one thing with another. Simile spotting is easy – all similes include either 'as' or 'like'. Pedants will point to exceptions – 'faster than a speeding bullet' and 'smarter than the average bear' are both similes of sorts, while a phrase like 'mist shrouded the hillside' is technically a simile because it's a contraction of 'mist covered the hillside like a shroud'. That's as may be, but we are not at home to Mr Pedant. Stick with the idea that all similes include either 'as' or 'like' and you won't go far wrong.

Some commentators consider similes to be a subspecies of metaphor, a sort of poor relation grudgingly acknowledged at family get-togethers. This isn't fair: a simile makes a direct comparison between two things, whereas a metaphor treats

> **Definition**
> Simile: *A word or phrase that makes an explicit comparison between two unconnected items using either 'as' or 'like'. For example 'My love is like a red, red rose' or 'As useful as a one-legged man in an arse-kicking contest'.*

them as one. Having said that, there's one thing similes and metaphors *do* have in common – they're both intimately concerned with imagery, word pictures that say more about a subject than straight talk ever can. Similes in particular aid abstract thinking thanks to their remarkable faculty for creative association. This neat trick is behind all sorts of famous moments in art and science. William Harvey, the great anatomist, noticed that the exposed heart of a living fish worked *like* a pump to circulate blood. Man Ray noticed that Kiki's back looked *like* a cello and produced the playful, punning image of *Le Violon d'Ingres* in response. Newton realised that an apple on earth behaves *like* a planet in space – both subject to gravity – although whether the famous apple-falling-on-head incident ever took place seems unlikely (despite the great man himself describing it to friends on at least four occasions). No matter: in each case a visual comparison was all it took to make a momentous mental leap.

Writers have long relied on similes to explain things, express emotion and make their words more vivid and entertaining. Finding fresh similes to use in your own writing also means discovering new ways to look at your subject. There are, of course, an almost infinite number of similes out there, but they all fall into two broad groups – what we'll call *one-offs* and *sayings*. Anyone can coin a one-off simile (in fact we all do all the time), but it tends to be only the rich, famous or otherwise quotable who get their words of wisdom recorded in books like this. Simile sayings – think 'dead as a dodo', 'sick as a parrot', 'mind like a sieve' and 'run like clockwork' – are available to all. Let's take a closer look.

One-off similes behave exactly like their saying siblings – they compare and contrast by means of a mental picture – but because they're original they pack more punch. One-off similes can really raise your writing, adding extra impact that in the right situation can be devastating. Take this example from John Steinbeck's *East of Eden*:

'She leaned against the dining-room wall and smiled at her girls, and her smile frightened them even more, for it was like the frame for a scream.'

Now hear this from Robert Duval's Lt. Colonel Bill Kilgore in *Apocalypse Now*:

'I love the smell of napalm in the morning. You know, one time we had a hill bombed, for 12 hours. When it was all over, I walked up. We didn't find one of 'em, not one stinkin' dink body. The smell, you know that gasoline smell, the whole hill. Smelled like...victory.'

The simple little simile can render our language exhilarating, heroic, devious, insightful, touching, graceful, shocking and uncomfortable, sometimes all at the same time. This versatility makes the simile the Swiss Army Knife of business writing. If a financial analyst comments that, 'Investors are moving like a school of fish – where one goes, all go', we're left with a vivid impression of the herd (or should that be shoal?) mentality of the individuals involved. Similarly the sentence, 'Consultants act like pollinating bees as they move valuable information from one company to another', makes more sense in less space than a more literal description of the consultants' work ever could.

Incidentally...

According to a 2004 BBC poll, Duval's 'I love the smell of napalm...' is the most popular line in cinema history, coming ahead of Jack Nicholson's 'You can't handle the truth' (from A Few Good Men) and Marlon Brando's 'I could have been a contender' (from On the Water Front).

Another great example of the flexible nature of similes comes from Cormac McCarthy's *The Road*:

'He kicked holes in the sand for the boy's hips and shoulders where he would sleep and he sat holding him while he tousled his hair before the fire to dry it. All of this like some ancient anointing.'

Sinister and tender in equal measure. Then there's George W. Bush's comment on Iraq, uttered during a White House press briefing on 22nd February 2001:

'I have said that the sanction regime is like Swiss cheese – that meant that they weren't very effective.'

Well, quite. What all these similes have in common is that their impact is directly linked to their originality (or in Bush's case, absurdity). Original one-off similes like these are often highly quotable and form the basis of many a maxim. For example:

'Love is like war: easy to begin but very hard to stop.'
H.L. Mencken

'After three days, fish – like guests – begin to stink.'
Benjamin Franklin

And even:

'Scepticism, like chastity, should not be relinquished too readily.'
George Santayana

In each case the simile enables the author to make his point with unusual brevity. The key is the striking image created by the simile and the understanding this image generates. There's no point being coy; be bold when coining similes and you've far more chance of generating the impact you're after. Still not convinced? Try this:

'Inflation is as violent as a mugger, as frightening as an armed robber and as deadly as a hit man.'
Ronald Reagan

And this:

'Venice is like eating an entire box of chocolate liqueurs in one go.'
Truman Capote

While there's more than a dash of hyperbole (see Chapter 2) in Reagan's similes there's no denying the power of the resulting images.

So one-off similes – often part of reported speech or published writing – enhance the explaining power of their author's words and are eminently quotable. But a second group of similes – a huge hoard in fact – have entered culture in the form of popular sayings. Many have rich and interesting histories and do sterling work making our words mean just that bit more, as we'll soon see. They're just the sort of thing that could enliven an email or boost up a blog entry.

For example, you may have been accused of 'running around the office like a headless chicken', in other words doing much while achieving little. Clearly this simile refers to the disturbing ability of decapitated chickens to race around farmyards apparently ignorant of their own deaths. Few of us have witnessed such a chicken, but that doesn't stop the simile doing its job. Like so many similes (and indeed figures in general), it doesn't make sense but works all the same.

Incidentally...

On 10th September, 1945, Lloyd Olsen of Fruita, Colorado attempted to chop the head off a luckless Wyandotte chicken called Mike. He bungled the job and Mike survived for 18 months. The axe blade, scientists discovered, had missed the five-and-a-half month old rooster's jugular vein, and a convenient clot had saved the chicken from bleeding to death. Mike's owner fed and watered the headless chicken directly into his gullet using an eyedropper. Because Lloyd had aimed the axe so high, most of the brain stem was left at the top of the spine. One ear had also survived. Mike, it seemed, had lost the power to see and to cluck, but could still hear and think. Celebrity status was guaranteed when a manager took the chicken on a national tour, and his story appeared in well-respected news magazines Life and Time. It couldn't last. Like many high-rolling celebrities, Mike met his maker in an anonymous hotel room after he began to choke and Lloyd was unable to find the eyedropper in time to clear Mike's oesophagus. True story.

In fact a hefty percentage of simile sayings make little or no sense to modern ears, time and fashion having mutated their meanings. Take 'work like a dog'. When was the last time you saw a dog do a stroke of work? The canine life is one of unabridged idleness. This simile dates from the 1740s so perhaps it was different in the old days, although it seems more likely the old association of 'dog' with 'low person' is (or rather was) the logic behind this simile.

Then there's 'easy as pie'. While pie making isn't exactly the ultimate test of culinary competence, it isn't a complete no brainer either. Despite this, during the last decades of the 10th century 'pie' was a slang term for anything easy. So 'easy as pie' really means as 'easy as easy'. Glad we cleared that up.

Incidentally...

One pie that wouldn't be quite so easy to make, bake or consume is the legendary Denby Dale pie. It seems that every few decades the residents of this small West Yorkshire town are overcome with the urge to bake the world's largest pie. Since 1788 Denby Dale claims to have has hosted nine pie festivals and baked ten huge pies in total. The first was baked in 1788 to celebrate King George III's return to sanity. Next came the 1815 pie celebrating the victory at Waterloo (George Wilby, a Denby Dale resident who had fought in the battle, allegedly carved the pie with his cavalry sabre – let's hope he cleaned it first). These two were big, but the first really huge pie was baked in 1846 to mark the repeal of the Corn Laws. This monster was almost eight feet in diameter, two feet deep and stuffed with beef, pork, lamb and game. Next came not one but two pies baked to celebrate Queen Victoria's Golden Jubilee in 1887. In 1896 they decided to celebrate the fiftieth anniversary of the repeal of the Corn Laws (using the 1887 pie dish in a commendable example of recycling). The First World War victory pie was inexplicably delayed until 1928 (news travels slowly in West Yorkshire), while the 1964 pie celebrated a number of contemporary Royal births. In 1988 the ninth pie celebrated the bicentenary of the first pie and finally in 2000 the citizens of Denby Dale created the Millennium Pie, a meat and potato monster over 40 feet long and weighing over 12 tons.

Other nonsensical simile sayings include 'like shit off a shovel' (surely it would stick?), 'sweat like a pig' (most breeds don't), 'stitched up like a kipper' (they're dead, gutted, skinned and cooked, but never stitched), 'laugh like a drain' (plumbing isn't noted for its humour) and 'sleep like a log'. This last example works by comparing the immobility of a log with that of a sound sleeper, but why a log? Surely any stationary object would suffice. Interestingly, an English-speaker sleeps like a log but a German-speaker sleeps like a woodchuck or marmot ('wie ein Murmeltier schlafen').

Not all simile sayings are so asinine; indeed, some actually make sense. Take 'like there's no tomorrow'. It's a fact that mankind has been merrily prodioting tho world'o domioo oinoo, woll, thoro'o boon a manklnd to do the predicting. Yet rather than being Eeyore-like in its pessimism, this particular figure is rather jolly, for it implies 'with careless abandon' or 'without thought for the consequences'. Despite what they say, tomorrow always comes. You'd have thought that would be enough to convince people of the immutability of the universe, but not a bit of it. Doom mongers have been confidently predicting the end of the world for thou sands of years, although as Jesus pointed out in Matthew 24:35-36, no one knows the exact date and time of the end of the world:

'Heaven and earth shall pass away, but my words shall not pass away. But of that day and hour knoweth no man, not the angels of heaven, but my Father only.'

Nevertheless, Judgement Days were forecast for the years 992, 1260, 1265, 1345, 1350, 1381, 1420, 1533, 1534, 1537, 1544, 1588, 13th October 1736, 5th April 1761, 3rd April 1843, 7th July 1843, 21st March 1844, 22nd October 1914, 1918, 1948, 1972, 1975, 1989, 1994, and 1995 – all of which obviously didn't happen. And that's just Judgement Days. Second Comings were confidently predicted for January 1000, 1648, 1666, 1774, 1806, 1920, 1975 and 2002, with Second Great Floods expected on 1st February 1524, 20th February 1524 (a busy period), 1528 and 1st February 1624, although happily this seems to have gone out of fashion recently.

Let's stay smiling for another semi-sensible simile – 'happy as a clam'. Clearly this conjures up images of being 'pleased as punch' or 'grinning like the proverbial idiot', but we're left wondering: are clams noticeably happier than other bivalves? It seems this American simile, first recorded during the 1830s, began life as the far more meaningful 'happy as a clam at high water' – the implication being that when the tide was in, clam diggers couldn't practice their nefarious art. Freedom from imminent pre-dation was enough to make any mollusc merry, hence the simile.

Incidentally...
At one time it was thought clams (well, the giant clam tridacna gigas, or pa'ua as it's
known in the South Pacific and Indian Ocean) ate people. It's not hard to see why
– they can weigh up to 180kg and measure 1.5 metres across. So persistent was
this myth that US Navy diving manuals even gave instructions on how to free oneself
(by severing the adductor muscle the clam uses to close its shell). The idea of giant
clams grabbing unwary divers is utter nonsense – although certainly strong enough
there are no authenticated accounts of these misunderstood molluscs doing anything
of the sort. These days they're more concerned with staying off the menu of
Japanese restaurants, where their meat, known as Himejako, is considered a
delicacy.

OK – let's recap. What all successful similes have in common (apart from the ever-present 'as' or 'like') is the power to invoke a striking image, accurate or otherwise. The result might trigger an important creative leap or simply communicate a message that stays with the reader long after the event. Of course similes don't have the whole word picture thing to themselves, as we're about to find out.

METAPHOR
WHO'S THE DADDY?

Definition
Metaphor: *A word or phrase that makes an implicit comparison between two unconnected items without using 'as' or 'like'. For example, 'The Lord is my shepherd' or 'I'm just a love machine'.*

Perhaps the Big Swinging Dick of all figures of speech, the metaphor is a rhetorical flourish that makes a direct comparison between two or more apparently unrelated subjects. At its simplest this can be a sort of 'X is Y' type thing (for example, 'War is hell'), although generally a metaphor describes X as *being* or *equal to* Y in some way, such as, 'He looked distinctly sheepish'. In this example X (his expression) is described with superb economy by comparing it to attributes of Y (sheep-like facial qualities).

Let's have another example of a metaphor transferring the properties of one subject to another:

Colonel Kurtz: Are you an assassin?
Captain Willard: I'm a soldier.
*Colonel Kurtz: You're neither. You're an errand boy...sent by grocery
clerks...to collect a bill.*

No longer the Special Forces killer sent upriver to terminate Kurtz with
extreme prejudice, Willard is reduced to the level of domestic drudge
courtesy of three cutting metaphors. As well as being the stuff of superb
descriptions, it's worth remembering that metaphors make inspired
insults. Not that their use is necessarily base – quite the opposite in fact.
Another important function of metaphors is to express the inexpressible,
hence their popularity in poetry and the like. Use them well and difficulty
recedes as understanding dawns. 'It is not too much to say,' observed
Max Muller, 19th century oriental scholar and inventor of the term *comparative religion*, 'that the whole dictionary of ancient religion is made up
of metaphors', while 1960s psychedelic shaman Timothy Leary proclaimed, 'Science is all metaphor'.

Leary might well have said the same thing about business language.
Such stock phrases as, 'It's a dog eat dog world', 'Put your money where
your mouth is', 'Let's not beat around the bush', 'He's a pain in the neck'
(or indeed elsewhere), 'Don't burn your bridges' or 'That's a tough row to
hoe' are all pure metaphor. When Johnson & Johnson advertised a new
sticking plaster under the strapline, 'Say hello to your child's new body-
guards', the customer instinctively understood that they're saying this
new plaster is strong, reliable, provides exceptional protection and will
generally take care of their kids. It's all a lot more effective than just blurt-
ing out something like, 'this plaster works'. Likewise, when Jergens
advertised one of their skincare products with the strapline, 'Science you
can touch', it worked because the verb 'touch' isn't usually associated
with an abstract concept like science. The dissonance between these
two ideas is what gives the phrase its legs – good advice if you're in the
strapline business.

As we saw earlier, some confusion exists over whether similes and
metaphors are sufficiently different to warrant their status as individual

figures. As a general rule similes make explicit comparisons and are decorative, while metaphors make implicit comparisons and are practical – they aim to make a point in the most effective way possible. A metaphor can usually be expanded into a simile, and a simile condensed into a metaphor, so they're certainly related although that doesn't seem sufficient reason to ignore their obvious differences.

Fashions in metaphors change over the years. Today we prize short, pithy figures, but it was not always thus. Consider (if you can) this metaphoric smorgasbord courtesy of 18ᵗʰ century novelist Samuel Richardson quoted by Henry Fowler in *A Dictionary of Modern English Usage*:

> *'Tost to and fro by the high winds of passionate control, I behold the desired port, the single state, into which I would fain steer; but am kept off by the foaming billows of a brother's and sister's envy, and by the raging winds of a supposed invaded authority; while I see in Lovelace, the rocks on one hand, and in Solmes, the sands on the other; and tremble, lest I should split upon the former or strike upon the latter.'*

As this example demonstrates almost too well, metaphors are a means of introducing ideas and emotions from one context into another – so a raindrop becomes a tear, fear a black hole, and jealousy a green-eyed monster. These comparisons lend the resulting communication a creative quality, hence the popularity of metaphors in literature, poetry, lyrics and – if I had my way – business writing. Through strange associations, the familiar becomes surprising and glamorous.

By now you might be thinking metaphors are pretty useful things, and if so you'd be in good company. 'The greatest thing by far', wrote Aristotle in *The Poetics*, 'is to have a command of metaphor'. Alas, not all commentators have been quite so enthusiastic. The empiricist-scientific tradition took the opposite view and in 1651 philosopher Thomas Hobbes wrote that, 'When we use words metaphorically; that is in other senses than that they were ordained for, we thereby deceive ourselves'. Spoilsport. We know that Kellogg's Cornflakes can't literally be 'the sunshine breakfast', but so what? No one is deceived by this metaphor into expecting a bowl of highly charged photons for breakfast. Instead, like many metaphors, it's an exercise in economy and compression that helps us mean far more than we say.

Metaphors are supremely flexible and come in several tasty flavours. Consider, if you will, this excerpt from Shakespeare's *As You Like It*:

> '*All the world's a stage,*
> *And all the men and women merely players*
> *They have their exits and their entrances;'*
> Act 2, Scene 7

It's an example of an *extended metaphor*, or *conceit*, by virtue of the fact the theatrical image introduced in the first line is carried over into subsequent lines. Extended metaphors had their heyday in the 17th and 18th centuries (think Donne's 'No man is an island' and Shakespeare's 'Shall I compare thee to a summer's day?'). Incidentally, an extended metaphor doesn't have to use words: many films use extended metaphors in the form of a recurring theme or image to tell their story. Similarly you could say the user interface of a Mac or PC is an extended metaphor with its desktop, trashcan, folders and so on. Likewise the mouse, with its vaguely murine shape and ersatz tail. The lesson is clear: if you're stuck for a way to explain a new, unfamiliar or abstract concept, try reaching for a metaphor.

Now, what do these two metaphors have in common: 'The quality of mercy is not Buffy' (from *Buffy the Vampire Slayer*), and ''Tis deepest winter in Lord Timon's purse' (from Shakespeare's *Timon of Athens*)? Both are *mixed metaphors*, a frequently amusing figure that deliberately disregards the rules of language. Mixed metaphors combine two commonly used but unrelated metaphors to create a new, nonsensical image. They're illogical, paradoxical and strangely effective, as 'barking up the wrong end of the stick', 'no skin off a duck's back', 'don't rock the applecart' and indeed, 'sounds good on paper' make clear. They're more fun than shooting monkeys in a barrel. My advice? Use often and with pride.

Alas, pity the poor *dead metaphor* – once happily alive before it lost its figurative value through overuse and passed away in the process. They're (ho, ho) dead common: 'run out of time', 'foot of the hill', 'tying up loose

A MIXED METAPHOR IN ACTION.

ends' – in all these examples the metaphorical magic that once made the idea of a hill having a foot so startling has dissipated, and we're left with an unremarkable husk. Dead metaphors, by definition, tend to go unnoticed. Some commentators make a distinction between a *dead metaphor*, of whose origins most people are unaware (such as 'to understand' meaning to get underneath a concept), and a *dormant metaphor*, whose metaphorical character we're vaguely aware of but tend not to think about (such as 'break the ice'). I'm not sure the difference is worth a new term – dead metaphor seems more than adequate to describe any metaphorical cliché.

Let's move on. Consider this comic outpouring courtesy of *Blackadder*:

> 'This is a crisis. A large crisis. In fact, if you've got a moment, it's a twelve-storey crisis with a magnificent entrance hall, carpeting throughout, 24-hour porterage and an enormous sign on the roof saying "This is a Large Crisis".'

Such verbosity is a clear-cut example of an *epic* or *Homeric metaphor* – a much-extended comparison packed with extra details that aren't strictly necessary for the description to work. Interestingly, these truncated epic/Homeric figures also come in simile format. This example comes from Philip Pullman's *Northern Lights* and describes a battle between Iorek Byrnison and Iofur Rakinson, two armoured bears:

> 'Like two great masses of rock balanced on adjoining peaks and shaken loose by an earthquake, that bound down the mountainsides gathering speed, leaping over crevasses and knocking trees into splinters, until they crash into each other so hard that both are smashed to powder and flying chips of stone: that was how the two bears came together.'

From the sublime to the ridiculous. In an *absolute metaphor* (sometimes called a *paralogical* or *anti metaphor*) there's no obvious connection between the subject and the metaphor, for example that odd little phrase, 'life's a beach'. Absolute metaphors are surprisingly useful and punch above their weight by confusing the audience, causing them to stop and think. The result is a swift creative post-rationalisation as they search for some plausible way to make sense of your words. Absolute metaphors make you sound deep, philosophical and profoundly profound, for example, 'I am Jack's complete lack of surprise', 'I am Jack's delusional state', and 'I am Jack's inflamed sense of rejection', all from Chuck Palahniuk's *Fight Club*.

Time to drop another metaphor in your toaster and see if it pops up. 'Shut your noise!', 'Frying tonight!' and 'Pigs might fly' – all three are *implicit metaphors*, in which the subject is inferred rather than stated. These examples all work the same way – If the subject (in these examples speech, fish and disbelief) is sufficiently clear we can leave it to the listener to fill in the details. Rather creative and the basis of many a good colloquialism.

Last but not least comes the *complex metaphor*, a figure that piles metaphoric idea upon metaphoric idea until the desired effect is achieved. A typical example is to use the metaphor of 'light' to represent 'understanding', and then take things further by saying something like 'throwing light' rather than 'shining light' to make the whole thing more poetic and noteworthy. 'That lends *weight* to the argument' and 'The ball *danced* into the net', are both classic compound metaphors. Why bother? Well, all metaphor makes people think – that's how they work – so complicating a metaphor with additional layers of meaning makes your audience think even more. The trick is to keep your audience with you, as overcomplication can lead to confusion (although that might be exactly what you're after).

So – metaphors make comparisons, come in a variety of guises, and enable you to raise your descriptive powers to previously unimagined heights. But the rich world of rhetoric has plenty more tricks up its sleeve to help anyone looking to paint the perfect word picture.

KENNING
FROM BEOWULF TO BOXCAR DINERS

Definition

Kenning: *A compound expression with metaphorical meaning used to replace a more familiar word. For example, 'moo juice' for milk or 'grease monkey' for mechanic.*

Interesting one, this. Unlike pretty much every other figure of speech we're looking at, the kenning's roots are in Norse, Celtic and Saxon literature rather than Latin or Greek. 'Kenning' comes from the Old Norse *kenna*, meaning 'to know or name'. In its simplest form a kenning comprises two terms that when considered together generate a meaning neither has alone. The result is mysterious and beautiful, or at least intriguing. It's a sort of 1+1=3 thing.

If that sounds a bit murky, a few examples should help. Classic Old Norse kennings included 'spear-din' for battle, 'sleep of the sword' for death, 'raven harvest' for corpses, 'tree breaker' for the wind, and – gorgeously – 'brow stars' for eyes. In the Anglo-Saxon epic *Beowulf* the sea is called the 'whale-road', a lovely image you might like to consider the next time you're having a paddle.

Don't think for one moment that kennings are a mere historical curiosity. The derivative 'ken' is still used in Scotland to describe what a person knows or understands about something, and indeed some early kennings are still with us, for example the Old Norse 'vindauga' (or 'wind eye'), became the Middle English 'windoghe', which then became our 'window'.

Contemporary kennings crop up in conversations all the time, doing what they've always done and describing the ordinary in an extraordinary way. A good example is '*cannon fodder*', a kenning for military personnel (usually infantry) that emphasises their expendable nature. While the phrase 'cannon fodder' dates from the early 19th century, the concept of regarding the mass of soldiers as the food of battle was known at least as early as the 1500s. In Shakespeare's *King Henry IV*, when Prince Henry ridicules John Falstaff's pitiful soldiers, Falstaff answers that they are 'good enough to toss; food for powder, food for powder; they'll fill a pit as well as better...'.

Similarly, cocaine, scourge of sink estates and society parties alike, is sometimes referred to by the kennings '*devil's dandruff*' (in reference to its white crystalline nature and evil reputation) and '*Bolivian marching powder*' (on account of its source and energising properties).

Staying with South America, it was Pelé, surely the finest footballer of all time, who invented the kenning '*the Beautiful Game*'. It first appears in the title of his 1977 autobiography, *My Life and the Beautiful Game*. The

Incidentally...

The French writer François-René de Chateaubriand seems to have invented the kenning 'cannon fodder'. In his anti-Napoleonic pamphlet De Buonaparte et des Bourbons, *published in 1814, he criticised the cynical attitude towards recruits that prevailed in the end of Napoleon's reign: 'The contempt for the lives of men and for France herself has come to the point of calling the conscripts "the raw material" and "the cannon fodder"'. In a nice touch, the first series of* Blackadder *reworks this kenning into 'arrow fodder', showing just how flexible these figures can be.*

book's declaration reads, 'I dedicate this book to all the people who made this great game the Beautiful Game'. His initial caps, and rightly so.

More kennings to conjure with: *pencil pusher* (for desk-bound workers), *God botherer* (for pious types), *beer tokens* (for pound coins*), coffin*

Incidentally...

The more astute amongst you may have noticed that one of the great things about kennings is that they're easy to come up with yourself and lend instant poetic credentials to your communications. Many, although not all, end in '–er' as they imply action on the part of their subject. So a mother of young children might be a 'bum wiper' or a policeman a 'thief taker'.

dodger (for old persons) and *soap dodger* (for crusty new age travellers), *peace maker* (for anyone involved in conflict resolution), *better half* (for spouse) and *ankle biter* (for crawling babies). I love the idea of God, sitting in omnipotent majesty upon his heavenly throne, being constantly interrupted by the prayers of the devout. Like a harassed parent you can just imagine him thinking, 'Can't they bloody leave me alone for five minutes?'

During the 1860s, US firearms manufacturer Colt chose a disturbingly blunt kenning as the name of their new revolver: the *Widowmaker*. Not much ambiguity there. It's hard to imagine Colt's product marketing team making the same choice today. Interestingly, the term 'widowmaker' has been adopted by heart specialists for a condition caused by a build-up of cholesterol plaque within the left main coronary artery, which severely reduces the blood flow to the left ventricular heart muscle. This plaque can cause sudden death and is particularly common amongst men, hence the brutal honestly of this kenning.

A rich seam of contemporary kennings can be found in US diner slang. This verbal shorthand, developed to lighten the stress of the restaurant environment and help hassled short-order cooks, thrived in American diners, lunch rooms and luncheonettes between the 1920s and the 1970s. Here's a small selection: *bubble dancer* for dishwasher, *soup jockey* for waitress, *sea dust* for salt, *moo juice* for milk, *boiled leaves* for tea, *belch water* for soda, *dog soup* for water, *bun pup* for hot dog, *frog sticks* for chips, *cow feed* for salad and – cheeky – *maiden's delight* for cherries.

There are many more, all with the same unintentional Old Norse feel. Alas, the irresistible rise of fast food chains means this casual creativity with language is coming to an end as older cooks and waitresses are replaced by students looking to make a quick buck and soulless computerised ordering systems become ubiquitous.

Incidentally...

A true diner is a prefabricated structure, often with Art Deco styling, built at an assembly site and transported to a permanent location for installation. The word 'diner' is a naturally derived from 'dining car', and diner designs reflected the styling of railroad dining cars – hardly surprising, since decommissioned railroad passenger cars and trolleys were often converted into diners by those who couldn't afford a new prefab. The creation of the diner concept is credited to Walter Scott, a part time pressman at the Providence Journal newspaper in Providence, Rhode Island. In 1872, Scott began to sell prepared food from a converted horse-drawn freight wagon outside the newspaper's building. In doing so Walter Scott unknowingly inspired the birth of what would become one of America's most recognised icons.

Interestingly, while most diner slang terms are shorter and punchier than their everyday equivalents, some are distinctly longer – for example *dough well-done with cow to cover* (buttered toast) and *shingle with a shimmy and a shake* (buttered toast with jam). Gone but certainly not forgotten, a number of diner slang terms have passed into everyday use including *mayo* for mayonnaise, *BLT* for a bacon, lettuce and tomato sandwich and *java* for coffee.

Scratch the surface and many occupations have spawned their own kennings – they answer some deep-seated need to rename and modify the official order of things, a call you should feel free to answer. We saw the medical profession's *widowmaker* earlier, while examples from US railroad slang including *'bo chaser* (railyard policeman, where "bo' is a contraction of 'hobo'), *lightning slinger* (telegraph operator), *lizard scorcher* (dining-car chef), *nickel grabber* (streetcar conductor), *rag-waver* (flagman), *stargazer* (brakeman who misses his signals), *tallowpot* (locomotive fireman, named after the melted tallow used to lubricate valves and shine the engine), *weed bender* (railroaders' sarcastic term for cowboys) and *zoo keeper* (gate tender at a passenger station).

AND THERE'S MORE
OTHER DESCRIPTIVE FIGURES

Many and varied are the figures used to describe, visualise and compare. Beyond simile, metaphor and kenning comes a whole slew of picture figures including hypocatastasis, antonomasia, parable and allegory. A *hypocatastasis* is a comparison by implication. In the right circumstances it can have even more descriptive power than its close cousins the metaphor. For example, if my wife were to breathlessly exclaim, 'You're like a love god', that would be simile; if she purred, 'You're a love god', that would be a metaphor; but if in a moment of amorous extravagance she simply swooned, 'You love god!', that would be a hypocatastasis. As you can see, the simple little hypocatastasis is calculated to arouse the mind and attract the attention to the greatest extent possible.

Definition

Hypocatastasis: *An implied resemblance or similarity – or to put it another way, a comparison by implication. Closely related to simile and metaphor.*

Hypocatastases are alive and well in our everyday language. If you're struggling on to a bus loaded down with small children and heavy shopping and a stranger lends a hand, you might well say, 'You angel!' If someone lies and cheats you might say, 'You snake!' When someone is being overly hesitant, you might call them 'Chicken!' This combination of brevity and energy means hypocatastases make great insults – try some yourself: Bastard! Pig! Arse!

Definition

Antonomasia: *A word or phrase used instead of a proper name. For example, 'Ol' Blue Eyes' for Frank Sinatra or 'The Big Apple' for New York.*

Another often-visual figure is the *antonomasia*, which involves swapping a generic description or phrase for a proper name. The word derives from the Greek word *antonomazein* meaning, 'to name differently', all of which is a clever way of saying an antonomasia is basically a nickname with knobs on.

'The Iron Duke' (for the Duke of Wollington), 'The Bard' (for Shakespeare), 'The King' for Elvis and 'The Gunners' (for Arsenal) are all thoroughbred antonomasia, as are 'Your honour' for a judge and 'Your majesty' for a monarch. When Rumpole of the Bailey dubbed his wife, 'she who must be obeyed', he was employing an antonomasia. Confusingly, the reverse – a proper name used to replace a generic noun – is also an antonomasia: 'Quisling' (Norwegian fascist politician during WWII), 'Benedict Arnold' (US Revolutionary War hero turned traitor) and 'Judas' (perhaps history's all-time top traitor) are all antonomasia that suggest collaboration and betrayal.

These also work well as insults. This from US comedian Rita Rudner: 'When I eventually met Mr Right I had no idea that his first name was Always.'

Incidentally…

Some antonomasia are rather clever (or at least funny) – take 'Mr Mojo Risin'' for Jim Morrison, (although technically that's also an anagram) and 'Thick and Thin' for David Beckham and Posh Spice (courtesy of Popbitch). In fiction, the practice of giving a character a name that defines or suggests a leading quality of that character is also called antonomasia, such as Sir Sidney Roughdiamond from Carry On Up the Khyber and Austin Powers' eponymous sidekick Felicity Shagwell.

Moving swiftly on, *enargia* is the collective name given to a group of figures concerned with conjuring up the most vibrant (or at least specific) verbal descriptions imaginable. In fact enargia means 'vividness' in Greek. Enargia can be absurdly specific – those ancients certainly knew a thing or two about detailed descriptions. Take *peristasis*, a description of attendant circumstances, in terms of place, time, context, personal char-

Definition
Enargia: *The generic name of a group of figures concerned with ultra-vivid descriptions. A sort of 'reading is seeing' thing.*

acteristics and so on. Then there's *topothesia*, the formal name for the description of an imaginary place; *dendrographia*, the vivid description of a tree, and *astrothesia*, a vibrant description of stars. There are plenty more but you get the point.

The Rev Henry Peacham described enargia thus:

'When we express and set forth a thing so plainly that it seemeth rather painted in tables than expressed with words, and the hearer shall rather think he see it than hear it.'

He goes on to describe the goal of enargia to be, 'that the hearer shall think he doth plainly behold.' Spot on. Skilfully-drawn word pictures help us understand the world, get insight into character, appreciate ourselves and contemplate the infinite – what could be better?

Another fine figure with plenty of descriptive power is *allegory*. In its simplest form allegory is just a way of saying something beyond the literal. They're usually found in literature, although allegory is perfectly possible in any form of realistic, representational art – painting, sculpture and so on. Though similar to metaphor, an allegory is a description taken to extremes – they go on longer, they're developed in more detail and they appeal to some deep part of their audience's imagination. Think of allegory as a highly extended, nuanced metaphor.

Definition

Allegory: *A sustained comparison in language or a work of art that provides a meaning beyond the literal. For example, Orwell's* Animal Farm *is an allegory describing the aftermath of the Russian Revolution.*

Definition

Analogy: *A comparison on the basis of some apparent similarity, for the purpose of explanation or clarification. For example, making a comparison between a computer and the human brain.*

Closely related is the *analogy* – Greek for 'equality of ratios' or 'proportion' – a direct comparison that appeals to reason or logic in a way that highlights a similarity between two subjects. As US civil rights lawyer Dudley Field Malone observed, 'One good analogy is worth three hours' discussion', which is why they're so useful when trying to explain the apparently unexplainable, as Homer Simpson knows only too well:

'Son, a woman is a lot like a…a refrigerator! They're about six feet tall, 300 pounds. They make ice, and…um…Oh, wait a minute. Actually, a woman is more like a beer.'

They also add richness to language through their ability to conjure up powerful images, as Gloucester's famous line in *King Lear* illustrates:

'*As flies to wanton boys are we to the Gods; they kill us for their sport*'
Act 4, Scene1

Analogies have a wider and weightier remit than you might think. Indeed, it's been argued that analogical language is the engine behind many of the figures discussed in this chapter – after all, metaphors, similes and allegories all get their power from their ability to make comparisons. Phrases like '*and so on*', '*and the like*', '*as if*', and the word '*like*' itself all rely on the audience understanding a particular comparison. Analogy is important not only in ordinary language and common sense, where proverbs and idioms rely on comparison, but also in science, philosophy and the humanities. And you thought it was just a simple figure of speech.

IN A NUTSHELL
TOP TIPS FOR BUSINESS WRITERS

- Don't confine yourself to literal descriptions. Instead, bring your writing to life by creating word pictures, the more visual the better. For example, you might describe a brand of coffee as 'smoother than a tiger in a tuxedo and more luxurious than a cashmere codpiece'. Verbal sketches say more in less space than straight talk – important if your word count is constrained.
- Not only is imagery highly expressive; it's also highly memorable. If a reader can associate a mental image with a particular point in your argument then the chances are it'll stay with them for far longer.
- Be brave. Try to squeeze picture figures into even the most prosaic forms of business communication. The less expected an image, the greater its impact. Just chose your examples wisely. If it works your boss can't complain.

- To come up with the word picture, try to set aside your preconceptions and see the subject afresh. What would a child see? How would he or she describe it? Try brainstorming word associations using a thesaurus or set yourself the goal of writing for 60 seconds on the subject without pausing or taking your pen off the page as a way of overcoming your inner policeman.

CHAPTER TWO

DRAWING ATTENTION TO YOURSELF

FIGURES THAT EXAGGERATE, EMPHASISE AND ILLUMINATE

If the picture figures in the last chapter are concerned with conjuring up striking mental images, then the figures in this chapter are about talking tall. If your writing needs a certain extra something to help it stand out then the figures we'll meet here – *tmesis*, *hyperbole* and *pleonasm* – could be just what you're looking for. We'll also cast a curious eye over *redundance*, *parenthesis*, *parabole*, *epitasis* and *anabasis* – all top tools for making your point with maximum impact

TMESIS
ABSO-BLOOMING-LUTELY LOVELY LANGUAGE

If there's no-bloody-way you're going to do something any-old-how because that would be ri-goddam-diculous, then you're already familiar with the charms of the *tmesis*. A tmesis (from the Greek for 'cutting') is a figure of speech in which a word or phrase is inserted into another word for emphasis, comic effect or the sheer pleasure of messing around with words. In the world of work they're a great way of

Definition

Tmesis: *Splitting a word or phrase apart and inserting another word or space into the gap for dramatic or humorous effect. For example, 'abso-blooming-lutely' and 'In two words: Im. Possible.'*

drawing attention to something that otherwise might evade notice. The tmeisis first appeared in Latin poetry: Ovid's *Metamorphoses* includes the verb 'circumdare' ('to surround') split apart with an extra word inserted into it to create a new phrase, 'circum virum dant' ('they surround the man'). It's a particularly smart tmeisis as it creates a visual image of a man being surrounded by literally surrounding the word 'man' within the sentence. If that all sounds a bit lofty then a few examples will show how familiar the tmesis really is.

One of the most common (in every sense) tmesis in everyday speech, *abso-fucking-lutely,* originated in the US as a World War One military profanity (today it's much loved by *Sex and the City* character Mr Big). Close relatives include the sarcastic *'congratu-fucking-lations'* and the exasperated *'un-fucking-believable'* and *'fan-fucking-tastic'*. In each case the aim is, of course, to undercut the intention of the host word for amusing or ironic effect.

Does the insertion have to involve the f-word? Dear me, no. Think of *'fan-bloody-tastic'* or *'abso-blooming-lutely'*, as uttered by Eliza Doolittle in George Bernard Shaw's *Pygmalion*. Incidentally, the inserted bit can go between the parts of a compound word, it can split an infinitive or it can slip comfortably between syllable boundaries. Where the split occurs is important – it can't go just *any-old-where*. The perfect insertion point is directly before the stressed syllable – so *'fanta-bloody-stic'* is anything but, and *'absolut-bloody-ly'* is just gibberish.

A tmesis can involve the insertion of space or pause instead of a word, and a rich subject this space insertion version proves to be. Take this quote, uttered by a character in *Hill Street Blues*, explaining the consequences of sex with an even slightly underage girl: 'Three words. Statue. Tory. Rape.' By breaking the phrase up in a way that makes no real sense, the gravity of the charge is somehow increased. It's got a bang, bang, bang rhythm to it – you can almost hear the judge's gavel calling a court to order. By making a phrase strange, the tmesis makes it serious.

Here's a similar space insertion tmesis, this time culled from one of Peter Kay's *Phoenix Nights*. Max, the Phoenix Club's doorman, refuses to climb a ladder, explaining his reluctance with characteristic northern brevity: *'Two words: Falk. Lands'*. Film mogul Samuel Goldwyn (the G in MGM film studios) may have set the

Incidentally...

Interestingly the city in which Hill Street resided was never specified, the producers going so far as to obscure whether the call letters of local TV stations began with 'W' (the designation for stations east of the Mississippi) or 'K' (signifying a station west of the Mississippi). However, Renko's claim in a season one episode that he had 'never been west of Chicago' was one of many indications that the series took place in the Midwest or Northeast.

template for this particular tmesis with his own immortal, '*In two words: Im. Possible*'. Here Sam makes his point (and his tmesis) by splitting 'impossible' in two, while neatly teeing up his deliberate error with the 'In two words' bit. Again it's an emphasis thing – by introducing an unnatural split to his sentence he draws attention to his point and doubles its impact (and indeed his word count). As you can see, Samuel's tmesis is the perfect figure to use the next time you're troubled by some wholly unreasonable deadline.

In the world of the tmesis one writer stands out: Frederic Packard. By day Mr Packard was a mild-mannered Harvard professor, by night he wrote witty social commentary for *The New Yorker*. Such was his penchant for the tmesis that during the 1940s he even invented a new term for it – 'schizoverbia' – which is pretty appropriate when you think about it. Let's have some examples. Returning from a Christmas spent (or rather endured) with young children, he described it as, 'the most *jammed-up boree* I ever went to, and a house full of *chattering little boxes*'. One sentence, two tmesis – not bad going. Then there's his description of a friend with an important new job who was 'going in for the *highest damn falutin*' you could imagine.' Finally, Frederic declared his income tax return was 'the most *rigged-up marole*' he'd ever seen. All insertion tmesis, all with added emphasis, all good stuff. The '*rigged-up marole*' tmesis is particularly clever. Not only does it make clear Packard's belief that the tax system was unnecessarily complex, but the 'rigged-up' part also suggests an element of cheating and dishonesty on the part of the tax authorities.

Incidentally…

The income tax complained about by Mr Packard is a comparatively recent invention. The first true income tax was introduced by Prime Minister William Pitt the Younger in his budget of December 1798 to pay for weapons and equipment in preparation for the Napoleonic Wars. Pitt's new graduated income tax began at a levy of 2d in the pound (or 0.8333 per cent) on incomes over £60, and increased up to a maximum of 2s (10 per cent) on incomes of over £200. Pitt hoped that his shiny new tax would raise £10 million, but receipts for 1799 totalled a measly £6 million. After that it was suspended and reintroduced several times until it finally became a fixture in the financial firmament in the mid 19th century.

Back to the tmesis and its role as an emphasiser. A classic example is the mild slang curse *Jesus H. Christ*. Like so many figures, it doesn't make much sense, which is why it appeals to the contrary part of our characters. It seems unlikely JC had a middle name – in fact like everyone else at the time he wouldn't even have had a surname in the sense we'd recognise – these were adopted slowly starting in the 16th century and are still resisted in locations as diverse as Iceland, Tibet, Burma and Java. Instead He was Jesus of Nazareth. The 'Jesus' bit (variously written as Iesus, Yeshû or Yeshûa') is a Hebraic personal name meaning 'Jehovah Saves', while the 'Christ' portion is a Greek title meaning 'anointed one', which matches the Hebrew term 'Messiah'.

Incidentally...

So where exactly did the H come from? No one knows, although that hasn't stopped speculation a-plenty. The first theory is that it stands for 'Holy,' as in 'Jesus Holy Christ', which is certainly a possibility although it does seem like overkill. Another explanation is that it recalls the H in the 'IHS' phrase included in pictures of the crucifixion by early Christian iconographers. 'IHS' dates from the earliest years of Christianity and is an abbreviation of the name 'Jesus' using classical Greek characters. 'Jesus' is pronounced 'Iesous' in Greek, with the 'e' sound represented by the character eta, which looks a bit like an H. When eta was adopted by those unimaginative Romans, for whom an H was always an H, the strange extra character began to be thought of as Jesus' middle initial.

American in origin, *Jesus H. Christ* was first recorded in print at the end of the 19th century, although around 1910 Mark Twain pointed out that the expression had been in use since at least 1850 and was considered old even then. No matter; for some reason *Jesus H. Christ* survives, perhaps because the strong emphasis on the H somehow improves the rhythm of its host phrase. The tmesising of JC's name doesn't end with 'H' though; it's often extended for effect as in *The Blues Brothers* where Jakes Blues (John Belushi's character) exclaims, 'Yes! Yes! Jesus H. Tapdancing Christ, I can see The Light!'

Time for some light relief. In fact, some levity would be most *wel-diddly-elcome*. This tmesis is a classic Flanderism, as uttered by Ned Flanders, the Simpsons' nauseatingly nice next-door neighbour. Ned is a keen and persistent tmesis-er, inserting 'diddly', 'doodly' and assorted other gibberish into perfectly good words. Homer hates Ned (well, as much as he hates anyone) because he's jealous of his lawn, his pay cheque and his insufferable optimism. The Reverend Lovejoy isn't keen either, but for different reasons; he's fed up with Ned's genuine piety and non-stop requests for guidance. Ned's problem is that he's just too nice, living as he does by a personal morality based on, 'three Cs: clean living, chewing thoroughly and a daily dose of vitamin Church – well, that, and resisting all major urges'. So powerful is the cult of Ned that he even has his own tribute band called, naturally enough, *Ned Zeppelin*.

It's a thoroughly ridiculous band name. In fact you could say it's *ri-goddam-diculous* – that's certainly how John Wayne would have put it. This tootootorono fuollod tmooic uttorod by Wayne in an address to US Army cadets in 1947 (and later adopted by Austin Powers) – is just the sort of thing you'd expect him to say. Only The Duke, paragon of unreconstructed machismo, could tmesis in such a manly way.

Incidentally...

Born Marion Robert Morrison in Winterset, Iowa on 26th May 1907, John Wayne's parents soon renamed him Marion Michael Morrison for the bizarre reason that they changed their minds and decided to call their next son Robert. Clearly Marion isn't the name of choice for rock-jawed legends, so it was a piece of luck that his neighbours started calling the young Wayne 'Big Duke' because he never went anywhere without his pet Airedale Terrier called Little Duke. Not surprisingly he preferred Duke to Marion and the name stuck. As naming stories go, it is indeed ri-goddam-diculous.

HYPERBOLE
BY FAR THE MOST BRILLIANT FIGURE OF SPEECH IMAGINABLE

The tmesis exists to draw attention to a particular point, but when it comes to exaggeration I urge you to employ *hyperbole*.

Definition

Hyperbole: *Extravagant exaggeration for effect. For example, describing a mediocre act as 'The world's top light entertainer'*

Synonymous with overstatement and emphasis for effect, hyperbole is a figure of speech in which statements are deliberately over-inflated. Bigging it up, as the young people might say.

Let's have some examples: *'I nearly wet myself laughing'*, *'He's rolling in it'*, *'That file took years to download,'* and of course *'I've told you a million times not to exaggerate.'* All very colloquial, as hype (to give hyperbole its more common name) tends to be. On a more refined note here's Roman poet Catullus in a distinctly romantic mood:

'Give me a thousand kisses, then a hundred,
Then another thousand, then a second hundred,
Then still another thousand, then a hundred.'

That's 3,300 kisses in one sitting – quite a commitment.

Incidentally...

A common mispronunciation is HY-per-bowl, recorded for posterity in the song These Words by pop princess Natasha Bedingfield. History doesn't recall whether Natasha was being playful with her pronunciation or just plain got it wrong. The correct pronunciation is, of course, hy-PER-buh-lee.

As these examples make clear, hyperbole isn't meant to be taken literally (in fact that's the point) – instead it's used to show strength of feeling and provide emphasis, rather than convey information. For this reason poets, lyricists and other literary types find themselves hammering the hyperbole, although it's something we can all use given the right opportunity. The opposite of hyperbole is understatement, or *meiosis*, but that's another story.

The great Henry Peachum's take on hyperbole was that it enables us to describe the otherwise indescribable. Here's how he portrayed its effect in *The Garden of Eloquence*:

'A wicked man is wickedness personified; a virtuous man, virtue come to life. This one is more blind than blindness, that one more vain than vanity. Sweetness is sweeter than honey; bitterness more bitter than gall. Or the comparison may be with living creatures: swifter than the swallow, blacker than the crow. Or with the gods and goddesses: more beautiful than Venus; mightier than Mars. Or offices: more stately than an emperor; more hated than a hangman.'

Nicely put. Another take on hyperbole comes from Thomas Macaulay, the 19th century historian, essayist, poet, statesman and all round brainy person, who wrote that, 'It lies without deceiving', which sounds rather po-faced for something so innocently enjoyable. Then there's Francis Bacon's comment: 'The speaking in a perpetual hyperbole is comely in nothing but love'. He could have added 'and showbiz'.

Or indeed 'religion', for the Bible is a rich source of hyperbole. One of the most famous examples is found in Matthew 19:24 (and Mark 10:25, and Luke 18:25): '...it is *easier for a camel to go through the eye of a needle* than for a rich man to enter the kingdom of God.' A nice image, but does it stand up to scrutiny? Er, no. It used to be assumed there was a gate in the walls of Jerusalem called the 'Needle's Eye,' through which an unladened camel could squeeze if it sucked in its tummy and held its breath. Sadly no such gate has ever existed. The first reference to the 'Needle's Eye Gate' is found in the writings of Theophylact, Archbishop of Achrida in Bulgaria in the 11th century. Not one to let the facts get in the way of a good story, Theophylact had never actually visited Jerusalem. Even if he had it wouldn't have helped because biblical Jerusalem had been destroyed twice by this time (in AD 70 and 134–136) so the original walls were no more. Instead Theophylact did what all good storytellers do – he made it up. The result worked a treat – we're still using his little fiction today, such is the power of figures of speech in general and hyperbole in particular.

Staying with a Christian theme, Jesus was much given to hyperbole:
'First cast out the beam out of thine own eye; and then shalt thou see clearly to cast out the mote out of thy brother's eye.'
Matthew 7:5 (where 'beam' is hyperbole for a speck – or mote – of dust)

'If your right eye causes you to sin, gouge it out and throw it away.'
Matthew 5:29

'You blind guides, straining out a gnat and swallowing a camel!'
Matthew 23:24

All 100 per cent hyperbole. G. K. Chesterton went as far as remarking in *The Everlasting Man* that, 'Christ had even a literary style of his own. The diction used by Christ is quite curiously gigantesque; it is full of camels leaping through needles and mountains hurled into the sea.' Chesterton's adjective of choice – gigantesque – captures the spirit of hyperbole perfectly.

But there's a problem here. The Bible is the word of God, the Bible is full of hyperbole, hyperbole is perilously close to lying (as Macaulay observed), yet God is not a liar. This has troubled Christian thinkers through the ages. One of the ways they resolve this is to point out that hyperbole can also communicate the truth by exaggerating it, which is presumably why Jesus was so fond of this figure. It's a great explanation and one every business writer should remember. Take this chunk from the opening stanza of *The Concord Hymn* (1837) by Ralph Waldo Emerson:

> *'Here once the embattled farmers stood; And fired the shot heard round the world.'*

The Concord Hymn describes the beginnings of the American Revolutionary War. Someone, somewhere, must have pulled that first trigger. Of course the shot itself wasn't heard around the world (it probably wasn't audible two turnip fields away), but its effect certainly was. It's our old friend the literal/figurative thing again.

So effective was this particular example of hyperbole that the phrase, 'a shot heard around the world', is regularly deployed in the wake of assassinations. In Europe the phrase is often applied to Gavrilo Princip's slaying of Archduke Franz Ferdinand of Austria, the event that tipped Europe into First World War. In fact Princip fired *two* shots; the first did for Franz's wife, the Grand Duchess Sofie (who was sitting alongside her husband), while the second hit Franz. No one was much interested in what happened to poor Sofie, so strictly speaking it was only the second shot that was heard round the world.

Incidentally...

With his mission accomplished, Princip tried to kill himself, but the cyanide capsule his quartermaster in the Black Hand gang had bought for this purpose proved a cheapo imitation that simply caused Princip to vomit copiously. He then tried to shoot himself but was wrestled to the ground and disarmed. Found guilty of starting a world war, he was sentenced to 20 years' hard labour (being too young for the death penalty) and died in jail of tuberculosis on 28th April, 1918, weighing just 88 pounds. Ghoulishly, the actual bullet that killed Franz Ferdinand is on display in the Konopiste Castle in the Czech Republic.

On a lighter note, in 2006 the hyperbolic phrase, 'a shot heard around the world', was used by various US media channels as a wry description of Dick Cheney's accidental shooting of lawyer Harry Whittington while out quail hunting in Texas. Amazingly, it was the wounded Mr Whittington who apologised to Cheney for blundering into his crossfire. Doctors reckon there are 'less than 150 or 200' pellets left in Mr Whittington but they aren't planning to remove them. If that's all the accuracy they can manage, I wouldn't let them try.

Staying with comedy (if you consider the wounding of neo-con lawyers to be comedy, and I think we do), hyperbole underpins a certain style of humour you may recognise. Consider these classics:

'I'm not saying my mother in law is fat, but you have to take two trams and a bus to get on her good side.'

'I can tell when my mother-in-law is coming over; the mice throw themselves on the traps.'

or

'I haven't spoken to my mother-in-law for years. I can't get a word in edgeways.'

All three are clearly examples of exaggeration for effect – in other words, pure hyperbole. The king of mother-in-law jokes was of course Les Dawson. While Jimmy Tarbuck, Jim Davidson, Bob Monkhouse *et al* all had a good stock of wife's mother gags in their repertoires, it was deadpan Dawson who ruled the roost, and it's easy to see why:

> *'I saw six men kicking and punching the mother-in-law. My neighbour said, "Aren't you going to help?" I said, "No, six should be enough."'*

Born in Manchester in 1931 Les got his big break in 1967 when he won ITV talent show Opportunity Knocks after years on the gruelling Northern club circuit. His love of words manifested itself in comic monologues, deliberately hyperbolic to the point of pretentiousness but delivered with an absolutely straight face:

> *'I was sat at the bottom of the garden a week ago, smoking a reflective cheroot, thinking about this and that – mostly that – and I just happened to glance at the night sky, and I marvelled at the millions of stars glistening like little pieces of quicksilver thrown carelessly onto black velvet. In awe, I watched the waxen moon ride across the zenith of the heavens like an amber chariot towards the void of infinite space wherein the tethered bolts of Jupiter and Mars hang forever festooned in all their orbital majesty, and as I looked at all this, I thought to myself, "I must put a roof on this lavatory".'*

The coming of alternative comedy in the 1980s meant Les' club style fell from favour. In June 1993 he suffered a fatal heart attack, ironically while visiting his doctor for a check up. Naturally he was prepared:

> *'The wife's mother said, "When you're dead, I'll dance on your grave." I said, "Good – I'm being buried at sea."'*

PLEONASM
COULD YOU REPEAT THAT AGAIN?

Taking a step back for a moment, the verbose Les Dawson monologue quoted above is an excellent example of our next figure of speech specialising in exaggeration, clarification and amplification: the *pleonasm*.

As the Dawson quote illustrates, a pleonasm is a figure of speech in which the speaker uses extra, additional, superfluous words to make their point (rather like I just did). The idea is that more words mean more clarity, more impact and more understanding, so it's perhaps not surprising that the term 'pleonasm' comes from the Greek for 'excess'. The test for a pleonasm is simple: if you can remove words without disrupting the meaning you've a pleonasm on your hands. A closely related figure (so closely related that we're going to consider them as one) is the *rhetorical tautology*, where the same

Definition
Pleonasm: *Using more words than necessary to express an idea, for example 'totally unique' or 'true fact'. Pleonasms contain redundant words that, despite their name, can be seriously useful when it comes to clarifying meaning.*

thing is said multiple times using different words, hence their alternative name of 'doublets'.

Both figures exhibit a big dollop of redundancy. In the context of language, redundancy refers to the use of duplicative, unnecessary or useless wording. But here's the really interesting thing: these extra words aren't useless at all; in fact in some situations they can be essential. By repeating part of a message, redundancy makes it more likely the meaning will come through loud and clear, essential in situations where ambiguity or noise could get in the way of meaning. And there's more. A baby, busy acquiring language, faces a truly daunting challenge as he/she tries to make sense of the grammatical rules underlying what he/she hears. A good dose of redundancy helps said child get to grips with grammar through repetition of the important parts – the more opportunities to hear, the more opportunities to get it right. It's one of those cases where more is more.

Anyway, back to the pleonasm. It's often taken to mean a worthless, clichéd, or repetitive word or phrase, although as we've seen repetition can be far from worthless. Here is an example (or three) that make the point: *tuna fish*, *safe haven* and *free gift*. In each case one of the words isn't strictly necessary but adds emphasis and meaning to its partner (note that the superfluous word varies – tuna are always fish so in that example it's the second word that's redundant, while gifts are always free and havens are always safe, so in those two cases it's the first word). Conversational English includes a plethora of pleonasms – some phrases, some whole sentences: '*at this moment in time*', '*I saw it with my own eyes*', '*alternative choice*', '*absolutely necessary*', '*totally unique*', '*boiling* hot', 'ice cold', 'empty space', 'added bonus', 'ears pierced while you wait', 'end result', 'future plans', 'small speck', 'unconfirmed rumour' and 'past history'.

These are crystal clear examples of pleonasms; slightly murkier (but still just about on track) are redundant statements like, 'my prediction for the future' or 'face up to the facts' (you can't predict the past or present, and whether you face up, down or sideways to the facts, they're still facts). Here we stray into the area of Yogiisms – named after Yogi Berra, a real life mid 20th century baseball star who became famous for utterances such as, 'When you get to a fork in the road, take it', 'You can observe a lot by watching', 'Our similarities are different', 'We make too many wrong mistakes' and 'The future ain't what it used to be'. While not *explicitly* pleonasms, these examples exhibit a certain pleonastic tendency with their combination of redundancy and crimes against logic. They're certainly good fun and could liven up a monotonous meeting.

Then there's the closely related *RAS syndrome*, a special type of redundant tautology where *RAS* (Redundant Acronym Syndrome) refers to using a word that makes up an acronym as part of the abbreviation itself, thereby repeating that word. Prime specimens of RAS syndrome include 'ABS system', 'AC current', 'LCD display', 'ATM machine', 'HIV virus' and 'PIN number', where the word represented by the final letter of the acronym is repeated immediately after. 'RAS syndrome' is itself an ironic self-referential example of the phenomena it describes: there are two 'syndromes', which is why it's a redundant tautology. The request 'reply RSVP' is pretty much the same thing as you're being asked to reply twice. Finally, the world 'Sahara' means 'great desert' in Arabic (via Tuareg), so referring to that big, hot, sandy place in North Africa as the 'Sahara Desert' is totally tautological, meaning as it does 'great desert desert'.

The law loves a good pleonasm. A possible explanation for double-barrelled phrases like 'cease and desist', 'will and testament', 'breaking and entering' and 'aid and abet' is offered by word maven David Crystal in *The Cambridge Encyclopaedia of Language*. He states that doubling up like this (a sort of tautological belt and braces) was used in legal documents for clarification during the period of English history when the legal system used both Anglo-Saxon and French or Latin terms in parallel. When early court writers weren't sure if both words had the same meaning or thought that others might not have a clear understanding of the French or Latin versions, they included terms from both the Anglo-Saxon and the 'foreign' words side by side, just to be sure. So legal mumbo jumbo all came about through scribes trying to be helpful. How thoughtful.

OK. Let's summarise. Certain figures of speech use wordiness to great effect – the pleonasm and its co-joined twin, redundant tautology, are the main offenders. Closely linked are Yogiisms and RAS Syndrome phrases – so closely linked that we've considered them all of a piece. That's the way with figures of speech – they often overlap each other with only shades of meaning to distinguish them. With that in mind let's take a look at some more closely related figures that can aid you in the art of exaggeration.

AND THERE'S MORE
OTHER RELATED FIGURES

First up let's cast an eye over the *asteris-mos*, a figure in which an additional word is inserted to draw attention to what follows. Its job is to cue up the main subject of the sentence, subconsciously signalling that the listener should pay attention because some-

Definition

Asterismos: *Words that direct the listener's attention to whatever is coming next. For example, 'Verily, I say unto you', or 'Oi, listen here'.*

thing good is coming along soon. The Bible is full of this stuff: *'Behold*, the Lord God said…', *'Yea* though I walk…', and so on. Many conversational exclamations perform the same function, for example *'Like'*, *'OK'*, *'So'* and *'Listen up'*. Their value to writers lies in the fact they insert a pause – like a rest in music – in order to highlight what comes next.

Then there's the equally fine *congery*, a figure concerned with saying the same thing in different ways in order to impart emphasis, rather like this:

'He departed, he went hence, he burst forth, he was gone.'
Cicero

You can probably sense the comic potential of the congery yourself, and so could those clever Monty Python boys:

> 'This parrot is no more! It has ceased to be! It's expired and gone to meet its maker! This is a late parrot. It's a stiff. Bereft of life, it rests in peace, if you hadn't nailed it to the perch it would be pushing up the daisies! It's rung down the curtain and joined the choir invisible! This is an ex-parrot!'
> Mr Praline

So far, so funny. But turning to the dark side, we get *prolixity* and *logorrhoea*. Both are examples of when good pleonasms turn bad, often (although not always) invoked to confuse or misinform an audience.

Definition

Prolixity: *The excessive use of words, in other words, language that is wordy, boring and verbose. For example 'three blind mice' might become 'a triumvirate of murine rodents totally devoid of ophthalmic acuity'.*

Prolixity is what happens when more words mean less meaning, producing a diminishing communication return. The easy way to spot prolixity is to look for verbose descriptions, convoluted phrases, excessive use of similes or metaphor, sentences pumped up with pointless expressions and anything that states the bleedin' obvious.

Two examples, both from the usually punchy Raymond Chandler's *The Big Sleep*:

> 'She came over near me and smiled with her mouth and she had little sharp predatory teeth.'

She couldn't very well come over and not be near me. And what other organ might she smile with? Then there's:

> 'He walked slowly across the floor towards us.'

As opposed to walking along the ceiling, perhaps?

Business writers can use a form of the prolix to attract readers' attention and make them smile at the same time by absurdly over-describing a product or its features. A great example comes from ad agency Young & Rubicam in Singapore in a series of ads for Uhu's new super glue ('Sets in seconds!'). One features a simple shot of the tiny tube with the following words:

For best use:

Read all instructions. Wash hands. Ensure all surfaces clean. Turn off the TV. Turn off any music. Unplug phone. Get everyone else out of the room. Breathe deep. Quiet your mind. Make sure you get a good night's sleep. Do not consume any alcohol in previous 36 hours. Forgive your parents. Come to terms with your past. Accept who you are...

And so on for quite a bit longer, ending on 'store at room temperature'. Another version included detailed directions describing how to reach not one but three local hospitals, while the final ad of the series read:

Keep out of reach of:

Small children, the elderly, the infirm, your wife, your husband, your friends, your relatives, the easily distracted, the mentally challenged, hippies, yuppies, teens, tweens, luddites, drunks, the meek, that guy over there, that guy behind him, in fact all those people, guys with nicknames, guys who give their privates nicknames, girls who tolerate guys who give their privates nicknames...

Ending, rather sensibly, on 'pets'. All of which just goes to show that sometimes it pays to ridiculously over do it.

Highly abstract speech or writing that contains little in the way of concrete language is known as logorrhoea, often defined as 'an excessive flow of words'. There's actually a medical condition of the same name present in a number of psychiatric and neurological disorders characterised by incoherent talkativeness. In the sane and healthy, logorrhoea is often given a far more direct and earthy name: verbal diarrhoea. This certainly isn't a figure I recommend you use, but spotting the logorrhoea of others can be fun.

Definition

Logorrhoea: *The use of highly abstract language, often within an academic context. For example, 'The individual member of the social community often receives his information via visual, symbolic channels', instead of 'People read'.*

Much academic writing is beset with logorrhoea, especially that post-modern stuff. So pernicious is its influence that it has attracted richly deserved ridicule. A famous example took place in 1996 when a respected physics professor at New York University, Alan Sokal, published a hoax article in a US journal of cultural studies called *Social Text*. His piece, called *Transgressing the Boundaries: Toward a Transformative Herme-neutics of Quantum Gravity*, argued that quantum physics had profound political implications and concluded that, 'Physical reality is at bottom a social and linguistic concept'.

It was, as you can imagine, loaded to the gunnels with postmodern psychobabble. On the same day the article was published, Sokal announced his hoax in a second publication and the fur really started to fly. Incredibly, the editors of *Social Text* – who didn't go in for bourgeois, late capitalist hegemonic methods of quality control like peer reviewing – claimed 'its status as parody does not alter substantially our interest in the piece itself as a symptomatic document.'

The politically and socially motivated abuse of logorrhoea to hide the truth or manipulate public perception is well established. You could always use it yourself in a tight corner. Try this snippet from TV series *Yes, Prime Minister* for size:

Appleby: Prime Minister, I must protest in the strongest possible terms my profound opposition to a newly instituted practice which imposes severe and intolerable restrictions upon the ingress and egress of senior members of the hierarchy and which will in all probability, should the current deplorable innovation be perpetuated, precipitate a constriction of the channels of communication and culminate in organisational atrophy and administrative paralysis which will render impossible the coherent discharge of the function of government within Her Majesty's United Kingdom of Great Britain and Northern Ireland.

Hacker: You mean you've lost your key?

Finally, to round off and bring some semblance of order to the riot of larged-up language we've just endured, I bring you the *parenthesis*, a sort of cross between a tmesis and a pleonasm, where a whole sentence, usually included within parentheses, is inserted into another. So for example:

> *'Peter stood in the midst of the disciples and said, (the number of names together were about a hundred and twenty,) Men and brethren, this Scripture must needs have been fulfilled.'*
> Acts 1:15

Or

> *'Nothing is easier than to admit in words the truth of the universal struggle for life, or more difficult – at least I have found it so – than constantly to bear this conclusion in mind.'*
> Charles Darwin, *On Natural Selection*

Parentheses give the writer/speaker/whatever the opportunity to air a thought or concern that can't quite wait until the next sentence. It's a sort of quick aside in writing. In theory, a parenthesis can be any length, although the longer it is, the more likely it'll be labelled a *digression*. It's usually thought digressions are A Bad Thing, but isn't that a little harsh? Digressions make for richer meaning and as you've no doubt noticed, this book is full of

> **Definition**
> **Parenthesis:** *An intentional change of subject. A way of going off at an angle before coming back to the main thread (not to be confused with a subplot in literature).*

them – that's because they let me get some related subject off my chest without disrupting the overall flow. In Lawrence Sterne's *Tristram Shandy*, there's even a chapter called 'A Digression on Digressions', itself nuzzled up amongst many other digressions. These sorts of nested digressions accurately mirror the free flow of conversation, and so, far from increasing the formality of language, actually make it more human. Who wants to get straight to the point, anyway?

IN A NUTSHELL
TOP TIPS FOR BUSINESS WRITERS

- Breaking a word up at its syllable boundaries and inserting either another word or a full stop is a simple but dramatic way of grabbing your reader's attention. It's also an effective way to create a high impact header or catchphrase out of unremarkable raw material. Breaking a short phrase into a series of single word sentences can work equally well.

- To emphasise a point, try massively *over*emphasising it. Your audience will know you're not describing the literal properties of your subject, but they'll be equally clear that you are alluding to something truly exceptional. It's a curious process by which you can convince readers of a truth by deliberately overstating it.

- 'Less is more' is a key commandment when it comes to good business writing, yet there are times when 'more is more'. It's precisely because we are taught to reduce verbiage wherever possible that deliberate over-writing using the figures described in this chapter can work so well.

- All these techniques involve overemphasising for positive effect. But that overemphasis must be done with style if it's to work. In particular make sure your piece flows. Keep your original point in sight even if you're expressing it in several different ways, and don't be afraid to make unusual word choices to prevent repetition.

CHAPTER THREE

SAYING IT ANOTHER WAY

FIGURES THAT SWAP, SHIFT OR FLIP

Sometimes saying it straight just doesn't hit the spot. In fact, we're all inclined to flower up our everyday language given half a chance, usually for no better reason than we jolly well enjoy it. Far from compromising communication, this wantonness with words actually makes our speech and writing *more* effective, particularly at work. That's because it helps us touch our audience's heart, and it's in our heart, not our head, that persuasion *really* takes place – a theme we'll return to again and again. All of which leads us nicely into this chapter's figures: we'll examine *metonymy* and *euphemism* in detail, before turning our attention to the familiar *onomatopoeia* and the unfamiliar, not to say downright exotic, *synecdoche*, *amphibology* and *periphrasis*.

METONYMY

HOUSTON, WE HAVE A FIGURE OF SPEECH

Metonymy (from the Greek for 'change of name') takes one aspect of something and uses it to describe something larger, hence its Latin name of 'pars pro toto' ('part for the whole'). A few examples should help banish any residual bewilderment: 'Scotch' for whisky, 'hands' for ship's crew, 'a smoke' for a cigarette, 'Hollywood' for the American film industry or indeed 'Houston' for mission control. In each case, one particular aspect of something comes to stand for the whole.

> **Definition**
> **Metonym:** *A figure of speech in which the name of an object or concept is replaced with a word closely related to or suggested by the original. For example 'crown' to mean 'king' or an author's name for his works ('I'm studying Shakespeare').*

In a similar vein, when a harassed waitress exclaims, 'The Full English just left without paying!' she's not referring to a replete UK citizen who walked out before settling the bill, nor is she saying the breakfast itself somehow did a runner. Instead she's substituting one thing (the food ordered) for another (the individual who ordered it). Similarly, when Australian farmer Mike Hastings was confronted by a British TV crew in 2004 who informed him he may well be the rightful heir to the British crown thanks to some backstairs business in the 15th century, they unconsciously used the metonym 'crown' for 'monarchy' and all it stands for. When asked how he'd rule once he'd ascended to the throne (another metonym), the potential King Mike 1st regally replied, 'I'd put a keg on for the palace garden parties and some party pies instead of cucumber sandwiches for a start'. So much for national stereotypes.

Let's have some slightly more sophisticated metonyms to marvel at: 'Give us this day our daily bread' (where 'bread' stands for any food), 'England won the Ashes' (where 'England' refers to the team rather than the country), and 'The pen is mightier than the sword' (where 'pen' refers to the written word and 'sword' for war or violent confrontation). When Shakespeare had Anthony proclaim in *Julius Caesar*, 'Friends, Romans, Countrymen, lend me your ears', he was referring to a particular *aspect* of ears, namely their ability to hear, and in doing so minted a prime metonym. Likewise when Knorr Soup ran an ad campaign with the strapline, 'Knorr takes you on a kettle cruise of England', the phrase 'kettle cruise' stood in for something far more prosaic like 'soups from around the UK' and was intended to be interpreted along the lines of, 'We've soups from all over the country, oh and by the way you make them using hot water'. Although Knorr's line is hardly the stuff of advertising legend, it beats the longhand explanation by a country mile.

By now you might be thinking, 'Metonym/metaphor – both paint word pictures, what's the difference?' And yes, a metonym is seemingly similar to a metaphor – the difference is their function. Both involve the substitution of one term for another – with a metaphor this substitution is based on similarity, while with a metonym the substitution is based on contiguity and/or association. A metaphor's job is to create understanding via comparison; the function of a metonym is simply to provide a point of reference. When we use a metonym we don't consciously aim to transfer qualities from one item to another as we do with a metaphor – there's nothing literally press-like about reporters or crown-like about a monarch, yet 'the press' and 'the crown' are both common metonyms.

In all the examples I've shown so far, the metonyms are fairly clear. Things get richer, more complex and more poetic when the metonym works by substituting an adjective for the more usual verb or noun. Strictly speaking, this changes the figure of speech into a *catachresis*, a sort of special case metonym (not so special as to deserve its own section, mind). Catachreses bend the rules of substitution described above but to rather good effect. They're still about swapping one word for another, but they work by introducing a word or phrase so far removed from the usual context or expectation that we can't help but notice. The substitution jars on our ears, but jars well, and that's its appeal.

A good example is the phrase 'the cold war'. On the face of it, wars don't have temperatures; instead they usually have names – Roses, Great, Falklands and so on. Swapping the expected noun for an adjective makes us prick up our linguistic ears, which is of course the whole point. The term 'cold war' was first used by George Orwell in a cheery essay called '*You and the Atomic Bomb*', which first appeared in October 1945. In it, Orwell talked of living in the permanent shadow of nuclear war and warned of a 'peace that is no peace', which he described as a 'cold war'. However, he stopped short of using his new phrase to describe the newly established stand-off between the Soviet Union and the West. That honour goes to US presidential adviser, Wall Street fat cat and all-round egomaniac Bernard Baruch. In April 1947 he gave a speech on the deteriorating international situation which included the sentence, 'Let us not be deceived: we are today in the midst of a cold war.' The term was instantly embraced by American media as an apt description of the situation between the United States and the Soviet Union: a conflict without fighting or bloodshed, but a conflict nonetheless. Later that year influential American writer, journalist and political commentator Walter Lippmann published a book called '*Cold War: A Study in US Foreign Policy*' in which he spelt out his belief in the need to respect a Soviet sphere of influence in Europe, so the phrase had clearly caught on by then.

Incidentally...

Conventional wisdom puts the kick-off of the Cold War immediately after the final whistle of the Second World War, although there's growing acceptance among historians that it stretches back to the mid 19th century and the tension between the Russian and British Empires that sparked The Great Game, a series of geopolitical shenanigans in Central Asia, and particularly Afghanistan, described in Rudyard Kipling's 1901 novel Kim. Interestingly it seems The Great Game was all a bit one-sided. The Russians don't have any equivalent phrase, nor do they have much interest in the whole business – history reveals the scheming and machinations were much more to do with Victorian imperialism and rampant Russophobia than actual events or real threats. True, there was one Franco-Russian attempt to invade the sub-continent called The Indian March of Paul but that fizzled out following the assassination of Emperor Paul I of Russia in March 1801 (although it's also possible that opposition to the adventure and even the assassination itself were somehow supported by the beastly Brits). In any case, Czarist troops never got within a thousand miles of the Khyber Pass (epicentre of all things Great Game-ish) so even the most bristling Colonel Blimp would be hard pushed to describe Russia as an imminent threat to the Raj.

Back to metonymy. The Bible is bursting with examples: 'He is the one who will build a house for me, and I will establish his throne forever.' (1 Chronicles. 17:12) where the idea of 'Kingship' is replaced by the word 'throne'. Then there's Genesis 25:23, 'And the Lord said unto her, two nations are in thy womb'. Must have been tight in there.

Galatians 5:16 yields 'the lust of the flesh' and 2 Peter 2:14 describes 'eyes full of adultery'. Mark 3:25 offers us, 'If a house is divided against itself, that house cannot stand', while Psalm 72:9 says, 'His enemies shall lick the dust' and Genesis 11:1 suggests, 'The whole earth was of one lip'. I'm sure you're already ahead of me in identifying 'house' as 'nation', 'lick' as 'lie face down in', and 'lip' as 'voice'. Once you get your eye in, metonyms are easy and pleasing to spot.

The Reverend Peacham had this to say on the subject:

'Metonimia is a forme of speech, wherby the Orator putteth one thing for another, which by nature are nigh knit together. The use of this figure is very great and very pleasant, it yieldeth great varietie of speech, and

serveth aptly to brevity, it is of large and ample capactitie to containe matters of great signification, and of many figures there are none more pleasant or more.'

He goes on to mention that metonymy is good for substituting:
'...the inventer for the thing invented: as Mars for warre, Ceres for fruit, Bacchus for wine, Vulcane for fire, Mercurie for eloquence.'

It's an excellent point. If 'Mars' can stand for all war and 'Bacchus' for all wine, then presumably 'Biro' can stand for all ballpoint pens, 'Hoover' for all vacuum cleaners and 'Xerox' for all photocopiers. All three are examples of a trade name achieving generic status and passing into everyday language. In Hoover and Xerox's case they've also become verbs – I don't know about you, but I hoover the house rather than vacuum it. Search engine behemoth Google was recently in the news for firing off a series of legal letters to media organisations warning them against using its name as a verb. The whole thing is both astonishingly po-faced and a clear stable door/horse bolted situation, as both the *Oxford English Dictionary* and *Merriam-Webster's Collegiate Dictionary*, America's leading reference book, already include the verb 'to google' (with a lower case 'g'). Google's zealous legal team claimed they were worried about trademark violation, but if they can't see that achieving generic verb status demonstrates market dominance for their brand then they deserve to be violated. In a nice way, of course.

EUPHEMISM
FROM 'WELL-HUNG' TO 'WARDROBE MALFUNCTION'

We're all familiar with euphemisms whether we use the word or not – 'smallest room' for loo, 'food recap' for vomit, 'wedding tackle for...well, as I say, we're all familiar with euphemisms: figures of speech intended by the speaker to be less offensive, disturbing

Definition

Euphemism: *An agreeable word or expression substituted for one that is potentially offensive, often having to do with bodily functions, sex or death. For example, 'rest room' for toilet or 'lady of the night' for prostitute.*

or troubling to the listener than the word or phrase it replaces. If you find it hard to face facts, euphemisms are for you.

Technically speaking, if a word or phrase is employed as a euphemism it becomes a metaphor whose literal meaning has fallen away, although as I've said before we won't get too hung up on the technical side of figures. Greek in origin, a *eupheme* was originally a word or phrase used in place of a religious equivalent that couldn't be spoken aloud, in other words, a taboo word. Interestingly, the opposite of a eupheme was a *blaspheme* (or 'evil-speaking').

Euphemisms can be slippery customers. Words that were once perfectly good (or bad, depending on your point of view), euphemisms themselves become taboo over time through a process the linguist Steven Pinker has called the 'euphemism treadmill'. So 'idiot' or 'moron' – once standard medical terms to describe delayed mental development – were replaced by the euphemism 'mentally retarded', which itself then acquired a pejorative feel and so was replaced by 'mentally challenged' and finally 'special needs'. Likewise 'lame' became 'crippled', which became 'handicapped', then 'disabled' and finally 'differently abled'.

It's easy to sneer at this process because it feels horribly PC (something we'll get to shortly), but there's a more pressing problem with the euphemism treadmill. US comedian George Carlin has pointed out that the progression from 'shell shock' to 'battle fatigue' to 'operational exhaustion' to 'post traumatic stress disorder' has in fact normalised and undermined the seriousness of the condition. He argued that, were the condition still called 'shell shock', then it might be taken more seriously and sufferers more likely to be offered appropriate treatment.

Interestingly...

The word 'spastic' was once a straightforward description of someone with muscular hypertonicity. After an appearance by cerebral palsy suffer and children's author Joey Deacon on Blue Peter *it quickly became a term of playground abuse. Partly in response to this the Spastic Society changed its name to Scope in 1994; never ones to be outdone by a mere rebrand, the UK's youth immediately started using the term 'scoper' as an equivalent insult.*

This leads us nicely into the sombre, almost sinister, side of euphemisms. In his book *Words are Weapons*, writer Steven Poole makes the point that we can often get inside a politician's head by taking the time to unravel their 'unspeak' (as Poole calls it). As he says, 'Even the most brutal kind of euphemism teaches us valuable things about the mindset of the people who employ it'. For example, a phrase like 'ethnic cleansing' subtly portrays those to be cleansed as filth and implies that removing them is nothing more than an act of hygiene. It's got an almost spiritual aura to it, in contrast to the sordid reality of genocide the phrase more accurately represents. No wonder euphemisms are frequently created and employed to disguise unpleasant or disturbing ideas.

Not everyone is so dismissive of euphemisms. Here's what Quentin Crisp had to say on the subject in *Manners from Heaven*:

'*Euphemisms are not, as many young people think, useless verbiage for that which can and should be said bluntly; they are like secret agents on a delicate mission, they must airily pass by a stinking mess with barely so much as a nod of the head. Euphemisms are unpleasant truths wearing diplomatic cologne.*'

All of which is very eloquent, but I can't help feeling Mr Crisp is just phrasemaking with his 'diplomatic cologne'. The trouble is it's all too easy to slip into twee territory, as Henry Peacham's comment on euphemisms from *The Garden of Eloquence* makes clear:

'*As the use of this figure is both profitable & pleasant, being artificially framed: so is it very unseemly and ridiculous, if Art be neglected.*'

So although euphemisms may not *offend* 'if Art be neglected', they can certainly frustrate, as these lines from *The Simpsons* makes clear:

Mr Prince: *We'll see you when you get back from image enhance-
                ment camp.*

Martin Prince: *Spare me your euphemisms! It's fat camp, for Daddy's
                chubby little secret!*

And this:

> *Judge:*   *Councillor, please refer to it as "murder", not "thinning out the herd".*

You get the idea. In real life euphemisms are regularly employed to substitute an agreeable – or at least non-offensive – expression for one whose plainer meaning might be harsh or unpleasant. For example:

> *'For 50 years, more women have trusted the special moments in their lives to Tampax.'*

The South Yorkshire equivalent of 'special moments in their lives' is the marvellous 'Rotherham are playing at home'. Do I need to mention that Rotherham's strip is bright red?

Then there's this grisly (and indeed huge) sentence from Tom Wolf's *The Right Stuff*:

> *'When the final news came, there would be a ring at the front door – a wife in this situation finds herself staring at the front door as if she no longer owns it or controls it – and outside the door would be a man come to inform her that unfortunately something has happened out there, and her husband's body now lies incinerated in the swamps or the pines or the palmetto grass, "burned beyond recognition", which anyone who had been around an air base very long (fortunately Jane had not) realized was quite an artful euphemism to describe a human body that now looked like an enormous fowl that has burned up in a stove, burned a blackish brown all over, greasy and blistered, fried, in a word, with not only the entire face and all the hair and the ears burned off, not to mention all the clothing, but also the hands and feet, with what remains of the arms and legs bent at the knees and elbows and burned into absolutely rigid angles, burned a greasy blackish brown like the bursting body itself, so that this husband, father, officer, gentleman, this ornamentum of some mother's eye, His Majesty the Baby of just twenty-odd years back, has been reduced to a charred hulk with wings and shanks sticking out of it.'*

That's quite enough unpleasantness; let's move on to something more uplifting.

As usual The Bible, particularly the King James Version, is a fine source of figures of speech thanks in large part to the solid Classical education its 17th century translators received. Naturally it contains its fair share of euphemisms. For example, in Genesis 4:1 we learn that:

'Adam lay with his wife Eve, and she became pregnant and gave birth to Cain'.

Along with 'lay' or 'lie', the other great biblical euphemism for sex is 'know', as in Genesis 19:8:

'I have two daughters which have not known man'

It's not just sex; the other great biblical taboo is bodily functions. Try this for size from Judges 3:24:

'After he had gone, the servants came and found the doors of the upper room locked. They said, "he must be relieving himself in the inner room of the house."'

Even better than 'relieving' is 'covering one's feet', a Hebrew euphemism for defecation, as seen in 1 Samuel 24:4:

'And he came to the sheep-cotes by the way, where was a cave, and Saul went in to cover his feet.'

Some people might consider this a euphemism too far, obscuring as it does the meaning of the passage. To address this problem one US translation from 1971 delightfully reworked this as 'Saul went in to a cave to go to the bathroom'. Well appointed, those biblical caves.

Confusingly, in biblical texts 'foot' or 'feet' can also refer to mail genitals, so that 'hair of the feet' is pubic hair (Isa 7:20) and:

'She came softly, and uncovered his feet, and laid her down' (Ruth 3:7)

Even more confusingly, sometimes feet are just feet (as Freud might say):
'How beautiful are the feet of those who bring good news' (Romans 10:15)

Historically, euphemisms for God and Jesus such as 'gosh' and 'gee' were used by Christians to avoid taking the name of the Lord in vain – something that would violate number six of the Ten Commandments.

Incidentally...

The Ten Commandments are listed three times in The Bible*: twice in Exodus (20:2-17 and 34:11-27) and once in Deuteronomy (5:6-21). The First Exodus and Deuteronomy versions (known as the Ethical Decalogue) are both consistent and familiar; the second Exodus listing (called the Ritual Decalogue) goes off the rails and starts rambling on about how 'The firstborn of a donkey you shall redeem with a lamb, or if you will not redeem it you shall break its neck', and 'You shall not boil a kid in its mother's milk'.*

At the other end of the scale, euphemisms for hell, damnation and the Devil are often used to avoid invoking the power of Satan and all his little wizards. A 19th century version was 'what the dickens' which doesn't refer to the famed British writer of that name but rather a contemporary euphemism for the Devil. In the *Harry Potter* books, the evil wizard Lord Voldemort is usually referred to as 'He Who Must Not Be Named', or 'You-Know-Who' (although Dumbledore is having none of it – in the first book of the series he thunders that, 'Fear of a name only increases fear of the thing itself'). Likewise John Mortimer's aging barrister Rumpole refers to his wife as 'she who must be obeyed', often shortened to 'SWMBO' and a reference to the novel *She* by H. Rider Haggard. The equally marvellous Arthur Daley had an equivalent in ''er indoors' – although frequently mentioned, 'er never appeared in the series although actress Claire Davenport – who specialised in fearsome matriarchs – did play her sister in the episode *From Fulham with Love*. Similarly, when luvvies refer to Macbeth as 'The Scottish Play' they're doing much the same thing.

From the sacred to the profane. This quote from TV's *Queer as Folk* is composed almost entirely of sexual euphemisms:

'I'm queer, I'm gay, I'm homosexual, I'm a poof, I'm a poofter, I'm a ponce, I'm a bum boy, batty boy, backside artist, bugger, I'm bent, I am that arse bandit, I lift those shirts, I'm a faggot-arsed, tudgepackin', shitstabbin' uphill gardener. I dine at the downstairs restaurant, I dance at the other end of the ballroom.'

Incidentally...

Both SWMBO and 'er indoors are examples of unseen characters, a common device in drama from 1970s TV series to the classics. Rosaline in Romeo and Juliet *is often spoken of but has no direct presence in the play, although she's clearly visible in the 1954 and 1968 movie versions. Amusingly, the plot of the play Bunbury, by Tom Jacobson involves numerous unseen characters from drama – including Rosaline from* Romeo and Juliet, *the boy from* A Streetcar Named Desire, *and Godot from* Waiting for Godot *– who team up to change the endings of famous pieces of literature, and, ultimately, history. Bunbury himself is not technically an unseen character; instead he's an imaginary character in* The Importance of Being Earnest.

Foreign words (think *derrière* or *faux pas*), acronyms (*VD*, *BO*, *WC* or *WTF*) and abstractions (*gone to a better place*) are all popular sources of euphemisms. Deliberate mispronunciations (as in *darn* or *shoot*) and indirections (such as *smallest room, unmentionables, privates, go to the bathroom* or *sleep together*) also work well. Lastly, technical terms (for example *copulate, perspire, urinate* or *prophylactic*) can always be relied upon for a euphemistic escape route if you're in a tight corner, as this snippet from *Pirates of the Caribbean* makes clear:

Will: We're going to steal the ship? That ship?

Jack: Commandeer. We're going to commandeer that ship. Nautical term.

Doctors' notes are alleged to be an excellent source of euphemistic acronyms. Examples include NFN (Normal for Norfolk), FLK (Funny Looking Kid), GROLIES (Guardian Reader Of Low Intelligence in Ethnic Skirt), GLM

(Good Looking Mum), GPO (Good for Parts Only), TEETH (Tried Everything Else, Try Homeopathy) and the marvellous UBI (Unexplained Beer Injury). DBI refers to 'Dirt Bag Index' and is apparently based on multiplying the number of tattoos the patient is sporting by the number of teeth they're missing to give an estimate of the number of days since the patient last bathed.

CALCULATING THE DBI.

Incidentally...

A figure closely related to euphemism, litotes, (or deliberate understatement) gives us the euphemistically inclined 'not exactly thin' for 'fat', 'not unattractive' for 'pretty', 'you're not wrong' for 'you're right'. Litotes can depend on intonation and emphasis; for example, the phrase 'not bad' can be said in such a way as to mean anything from 'mediocre' to 'excellent'.

Moving away from acronyms, 'Digging for worms' is varicose vein surgery, 'Departure lounge' Is a geriatric ward and 'Handbag positive' refers to the sad sight of a confused elderly lady lying on a hospital bed clutching her handbag. Finally, TTFO is the slightly uncharitable, 'Told to Fuck Off' (or 'To Take Fluids Orally' if the Registrar is looking).

What of euphemisms in the world of work? Well, there's 'in-store wastage' for shoplifting, 'creative accountancy' for borderline financial fraud and 'expression of trade union solidarity' for picket line mob, the latter lovingly coined in the 1970s heyday of industrial action. Nigel Rees, Radio 4's long-time language expert, tells the story of a Westminster local government official who in 1944 apparently decided that the council's 'rat-catcher' should be known henceforward as a 'rodent officer'. This, in turn, became the even more rarefied 'rodent operative' and 'rodent operator' (which, as Rees points out, raises the ticklish question of how exactly does one operate a rodent?) Rees calls this process 'job title enhancement', itself a euphemism for a process many of us might reasonably describe as 'snobbery'.

Incidentally...
Shortly before the Second World War US man of letters H. L. Mencken playfully proposed the euphemism 'ecdysis' (inspired by the Greek for 'I take off') for 'stripper'. The only problem is that the word ecdysis already had a perfectly good role – describing the shedding of outer layers of skin by snakes, crustaceans and insects. The famous stripper, Gypsy Rose Lee, was scandalised – perhaps for the first time in her life. In a 1940 interview, she levelled her guns against Mencken: 'Ecdysiast, he calls me! Why, the man has been reading books! Dictionaries! We don't wear feathers and molt them off! What does he know about stripping?'

In *A Better Class of Person*, playwright John Osborne famously recalled how his mother would roundly declare to anyone who was listening: 'I'm not a barmaid. I'm a victualler's assistant.' Likewise the Scarborough branch of the now defunct Safeway supermarket chain felt able to advertise for an 'ambient replenishment assistant' rather than a shelf stacker. We may laugh, but the far from amusing result of this nonsense is an erosion of precision in language. In recent years we've seen 'appearance engineer', 'customer operations leader', and 'utensil sanitation manager' for hairdresser, train guard and dishwasher respectively. All real job descriptions. My favourite has to be the pleasingly tongue-in-cheek (although still absolutely genuine) 'digital scatologist', a software engineer assigned to analyse what are technically known as 'memory dumps', a recording of a computer's memory the moment it crashed used for debugging purposes. 'Digital scatologist' lends this most tedious of technical jobs a nice edge.

Euphemism in the workplace doesn't end with job descriptions. It scales a particularly pusillanimous peak at the other end of the work process: in dismissal. Sir Alan Sugar's shtick,'You're fired!' may have caught on in the media and popular culture but it's rarely heard in the workplace itself. In fact, managers still go to extraordinary lengths to let employees down gently at the point of departure. This may be because they want to lessen the blow but equally it may be because they just can't bring themselves to be blunt about such a painful matter. Euphemisms for redundancy include, 'career change opportunity', 'deselected' (also the fate of those in public office, along with the timeless 'spend more time with one's family' and 'give time to one's other commitments'), 'natural wastage', 'decruitment', 'downsizing', 'being let go', 'negotiated departure', 'rationalisation', 'restructuring', 'workforce imbalance correction' and the delightful 'involuntarily leisured'. As Rees points out, the whole business is enough to drive a man to beverages.

What powers this bizarre process of euphemising? Clearly there's an element of the aforementioned fear and snobbery, plus a certain amount of self-aggrandisement and that modern demon, political correctness. A surprisingly large number of businesses seem curiously concerned with protecting the tender feelings of their workers (who, it should be pointed out, mostly don't give a monkey's what their job is called as long as they've got one). PC is, of course, an easy target, but I don't see why that should stop us putting the boot in. A recent example was the rewriting of the old sea shanty *What Shall We Do With The Drunken Sailor?* as *What Shall We Do With The Grumpy Pirate?* The idea was to remove any reference to alcohol. So, 'Put him in the brig until he's sober' was replaced by the insipid, 'Do a little jig and make him smile', while, 'Round with the rum and scotch and whisky' has become, 'Tickle him till he starts to giggle'.

All good stuff for raising blood pressure at the Tunbridge Wells Conservative Association, but it's not *quite* what it seems. In this example the lyrics were reworked for a one-off pirate theme day, not as a generic cleansing of anything drink-related. Likewise, the widely reported remix of the nursery rhyme *Baa Baa Black Sheep* to read *Baa Baa Rainbow Sheep* never really took place – what the kids were asked to do was come up with an action rhyme that involved sheep that were happy, sad, red, blue, bouncing, sleeping and so on. As satirical magazine *Private Eye* has reported, what's really happening here is the misrepresentation of basically innocent events by tabloids with their own bitter and twisted political agendas.

AND THERE'S MORE
OTHER FLIPPING FIGURES

One figure many people remember from school is *onomatopoeia*, although the chances are your teacher didn't describe it as a figure of speech. It is, of course, the choice of particular words to imitate natural sounds or suggest a specific source: 'sizzle', 'bang', 'oink', 'clang' and so on. The effect increases when multiple onomatopoeic words are ganged together, as in this lovely excerpt from Sir Alfred Tennyson's poem *Come Down, O Maid*, where multiple 'm' and 'n' sounds produce an atmosphere of lazy summer insects:

> **Definition**
> **Onomatopoeia:** *The formation of words in imitation of sounds. Onomatopoeia can also refer to the use of word sounds for rhetorical effect.*

> '... *the moan of doves in immemorial elms,*
> *And murmuring of innumerable bees.*'

Another name for this effect is 'imitative harmony', which is certainly a nice way of putting it. The word 'onomatopoeia' itself is the result of combining the Greek for 'name' ('onoma') and 'I make' ('poieo'), which sort of adds up to 'named after the sound I make'. Well, that's how I interpret it.

Like almost all our figures, this one has been around for centuries. In Henry Peacham's time it was the basis of much onomatopoeic name-calling. In *The Garden of Eloquence* he mentions:

> *'We calleth a woman who delighteth much to hear tales a flibergib, trish-trash, tagnag, hunch-lunch, riffraff, hadnab, heave and hoe, clap-perclaw, kickle-kackle.'*

Incidentally...

Over time the onomatopoeic word may evolve into an entirely new word, at which point it's no longer an example of onomatopoeia. One example is the word 'bleat' used to describe the noise a sheep makes. In medieval times it was pronounced 'blairt' (with a silent R) or 'blet' with the vowel drawled, both of which are clearer examples of imitative harmony than the modern pronunciation. An example of the opposite case is 'cuckoo', which, presumably thanks to continuous familiarity with the bird noise down the centuries, has kept approximately the same pronunciation since Anglo-Saxon times and hasn't changed to match the vowel sound of words like 'cuckold'.

One of the great things about onomatopoeia is its ease of use. We seem to be naturally predisposed to enjoy words that sound like the thing they represent. So deep is this connection that onomatopoeia was once thought to have some role in the origin of language itself, the so-called 'bow-wow' theory that suggests words originated as onomatopoeic imitations of natural sounds.

Now, before we get carried away applauding onomatopoeia for its crucial contribution to civilisation, I must point out that the origins of language are both utterly obscure and intensely debated. As Christine Kenneally points out in *The First Word: The Search for the Origins of Language*:

> *'For all its power to wound and seduce, speech is our most ephemeral creation; it is little more than air. It exits the body as a series of puffs and dissipates quickly into the atmosphere. There are no verbs preserved in*

amber, no ossified nouns, and no prehistorical shrieks forever spread-eagled in the lava that took them by surprise.'

Kenneally has described nailing the origin of language as 'the hardest problem in science today', which seems a little OTT given our various issues with the environment, food production, pandemics and so forth. That hasn't stopped speculation aplenty, although annoyingly no single theory can account for more than a small part of language. The aforementioned bow-wow theory says that language began when our ancestors started imitating the natural sounds around them. In other words, the first speech comprised 'echoic' words such as 'moo', 'meow', 'splash', 'cuckoo', and 'bang'. It's a neat theory, but grammarian Richard Nordquist has pointed out that relatively few words are onomatopoeic, and even the words that are, vary from one language to another. A dog's bark, for instance, is heard as 'au au' in Brazil, 'ham ham' in Albania, and 'wang, wang' in China. What's more, many onomatopoeic words are of relatively recent origin, and many don't come from natural sounds (anything metallic sounding for example, such as the mighty *kerrang*).

The other theories, in case you're interested, are the 'Yo-Heave-Ho' theory, in which language evolved from the grunts, groans, and snorts evoked by heavy physical labour, the 'Pooh-Pooh' theory in which speech began with interjections, spontaneous cries of pain ('Ouch!'), surprise ('Oh!'), and other emotions ('Yabba dabba do!'), the 'La-La' theory in which language developed from sounds associated with love, play and song, and the frankly batty 'Ding-Dong' theory as favoured by Plato and Pythagoras, in which speech arose in response to the essential qualities of objects in the environment. All suffer from one or more fatal error, but given these shortcomings I'm going with the Flintstones.

In the world of work, onomatopoeia does sterling service in the creation of memorable advertising slogans/straplines/whateveryouwantto callthems. For many years Alka Seltzer has promoted itself with 'plink, plink, fizz, fizz', while generations of school children have been introduced to onomatopoeia by stealth via the Rice Krispies strapline of 'snap, crackle, pop'. Back in the 1970s Jimmy Saville implored us to 'Clunk Click Every

Trip' as a way of promoting the wearing of seatbelts. This became 'click, clack, front and back' in Australia and 'click it or ticket' in the USA.

Staying with childhood for a moment, you may recall onomatopoeic sound effects in both comics, cartoons and the more inane TV shows. In particular the late 1960s Adam West/Burt Ward *Batman* series featured full screen 'ker-splatt!' graphics flashed up as our eponymous hero slugged The Riddler or whoever. These written sound effects were an integral part of comic book iconography. Marvel Comics went as far as trademarking two words of their own: 'thwip!' (the sound of Spider-Man's web shooter), and 'snikt!' (the switchblade sound of Wolverine's claws locking into place).

Let's move on. Earlier we met the marvellous *metonym* – now allow me to introduce its kissing cousin, the *synecdoche*. Here a specific part of something is used to refer to the whole. The difference between the two is subtle but important: when A refers to *and is a component of* B then it's a synecdoche; if A is commonly associated with B but *not actually part of its whole* then it's a metonym. Clear as mud. So 'Downing Street' is a metonym for the British Prime Minister and his staff, because Downing Street (A) is clearly not part of the Prime Minister or his staff (B) but is closely associated with them. On the other hand, '50 head of cattle' is a synecdoche

Definition

Synecdoche: *A figure of speech in which a part is used for the whole (as in hand for sailor), the whole for a part (as in the law for police officer), the specific for the general (as in cutthroat for assassin), the general for the specific (as in thief for pickpocket), or the material for the thing made from it (as in steel for sword).*

because heads (A) are indeed part of the cattle (B) referred to in the phrase. It's really about scale change – a synecdoche describes one thing in terms of another, but at a different level of magnification. Glad we sorted that out.

Let's have some examples: tickle the ivories, tread the boards and pay on plastic – in each case the noun is part of a greater whole. Similarly, and on a more street level, if I complimented you on your 'fly threads', praised the 'righteous grooves' emitting from your stereo and affirmed you had 'the baddest wheels in town' I'd be synecdoching with the best of them (as well as sounding disturbingly like a character from *Starsky and Hutch*).

In fact even a phrase like 'the word on the street' is itself a synecdoche (actually it's two – 'word' and 'street' – both are part of a bigger whole). In a similar vein, hands up everyone who remembers Australian songstress Helen Reddy's proto-feminist anthem *I Am Woman, Hear Me Roar*? By suggesting that she was a component part of some sort of universal womankind, Helen was serving up a prime synecdoche.

Going a bit upmarket, T. S. Eliot used the synechdochic phrase 'a pair of ragged claws' to describe a crab in *The Love Song of J. Alfred Prufrock,* increasing the sense of sharpness and savagery of the claws in the process. Other examples include, 'A land flowing with milk and honey' (Exodus 3:8, 17) and 'Give us this day our daily bread' (Matthew 6).

Perhaps the easiest way to think about a synecdoche is as a literary symbol; an iconic representation that carries a particular meaning. It's also a surprisingly important subject in the study of literature. US critic Kenneth Burke wrote in *The Philosophy of Literary Form* that, 'The more I examine the structure of poetry and the structure of human relations outside poetry, the more I become convinced that this [the synecdoche] is the basic figure of speech.' His point is that all language is made up of symbols, a view that has a lengthy backstory, starting with Aristotle writing this in his work *On Interpretation*:

'Spoken words are the symbols of mental experience, and written words are the symbols of spoken words.'

The word 'book', for example, either spoken or written, clearly isn't a literal book but rather a series of symbols rendered in ink on paper or pixels on screen that by convention stand for the idea of a book. In other words, the written or spoken word represents a particular concept in our minds.

Perhaps not surprisingly, given its hidden depths, the Rev Peacham included a caution about synecdoche in *The Garden of Eloquence*:

'The use of this figure is very unfit among ignorant hearers which for lacke of knowledge may mistake it, and likewise among cavilling and captious persons, which of wilfull perversenesse may canily pervert the true meaning, either by malice or mockerie.'

No wonder its Latin name is 'Intellecto'.

Next let's look at *amphibology*. If you've ever enjoyed the old line, 'time flies like an arrow; fruit flies like a banana', then you've already met an example of an amphibol. As you can probably guess from this example, amphibology is driven by ambiguity. In *Animal Crackers*, Groucho Marx remarks:

> *'I once shot an elephant in my pyjamas. How he got in my pyjamas I'll never know.'*

You can almost hear the drum roll and cymbal hit. This line works by virtue of the fact that the first sentence alone is unclear about whether the speaker shot the elephant while wearing pyjamas or whether the elephant was in the speaker's pyjamas. It's the same with the time flies/fruit flies line – the phrase works by playing on the ambiguity of 'flies' as either those little pesky insects or the process of something speeding along.

Definition
Amphibology: *A phrase susceptible of two interpretations and hence of uncertain meaning.*

Amphibological statements can make great straplines, although sometime it's not clear whether the humour is deliberate or otherwise, as these genuine examples taken from signage show:

> *Used cars for sale: Why go elsewhere to be cheated? Come here first!*

or

> *Eat our curry, you won't get better.*

or

> *No food is better than our food.*

Lastly amphibology can help you avoid saying something that might harm your chances of getting what you want, although it's far from clear if this is ethical. The classic example is a libidinous male who for ulterior reasons doesn't want to divulge his relationship status while chatting with a new female. In this situation he could use amphibological language to talk about his significant other without making clear if he's currently in a relationship. For example, instead of saying, 'She decided we'd eat out', he might say 'We decided to eat out'. It's sometimes called 'playing the pronoun game' and is equally useful in concealing sexual orientation in conversation by avoiding gender-specific pronouns for a partner or lover. When The Pet Shop Boys covered Elvis Presley's *You Are Always On My Mind* in 1987, singer Neil Tennant – who didn't come out about his homosexuality until 1993 – changed the lyric to, 'Girl, I'm sorry I was blind' to 'I'm so sorry I was blind'.

Finally in this chapter let's meet the *periphrasis*. It's the substitution of a descriptive word or phrase for a proper name, often at great (or at least greater) length, so you could say it's a species of circumlocution.

Politicians are often masters of periphrasis; they use it to avoid giving a straight answer. That sounds awful but in the right hands it can work brilliantly, as in Winston Churchill's response to a dumb question:

> 'The answer, sir, is in the plural, and they bounce.'

Definition

Periphrasis: *A roundabout or indirect manner of writing or speaking. In literature periphrasis is sometimes used for comic effect.*

This link to circumlocution means a periphrasis often involves using several words when one (or none) would do. At one time periphrasis was the height of linguistic elegance, so much so that fish became 'the finny tribe' and tea (according to Wordsworth), 'the fragrant beverage draw from China's herb'.

As such it's the enemy of clear writing and something you should probably avoid (unless you have the sureness of touch that Churchill demonstrates). In fact Struck and White's timeless 'omit needless words' is perhaps the best advice for any writer.

Let's have some examples. 'The fact that' is often used in combination with 'because of', or 'in light of', or 'in view of', or 'due to', all of which can be usefully replaced with the single word 'because'. So instead of saying, 'In view of the fact that I haven't had a shower this week, please keep your distance', it would be a lot simpler to say 'Because I haven't had a shower this week' (actually it would just be simpler to say, 'I'm a bit smelly' or better still, say nothing and just have a bath.)

Then there's, 'The reason...' This is usually nothing more than padding and has no place in good business writing. So, 'The reason he didn't win the contract was because he missed the deadline', simply becomes, 'He didn't win the contract because he missed the deadline'. It's shorter, faster and far more direct.

In a similar vein is 'Basically...' which, basically, is overused. So at work, instead of saying, 'Basically, it's because he's lazy', just say, 'It's because he's lazy.'

It's only a short hop from here to fattened up, unnaturally constructed, ornate sentences, such as Jonathan Swift's, 'I said the thing which was not', which is another way of saying, 'I lied'. Although fun to construct, in the context of business writing I strongly suggest you avoid such nonsense at all costs.

Outside the context of business writing this 'extra words' aspect means periphrasis is often employed in relation to sex, typically with a big dollop of euphemism and/or irony added:

'Your daughter and the Moor are now making the beast with two backs.'
Othello, Act 1, Scene 1

And

'Cunegonde saw Dr Pangloss behind some bushes giving a lesson in experimental philosophy to her mother's waiting woman, a little brunette who seemed eminently teachable.'
Candide, Voltaire

IN A NUTSHELL
TOP TIPS FOR BUSINESS WRITERS

- Think about the idea or action *behind* the obvious. Look for a significant *part* of the whole. What's the thing that actually matters or is most memorable when all the hoopla is stripped away? It could be a word or a sentence but whatever it is, make that the focus of your writing.

- Try euphemising utterly non-offensive words for humorous or eye-catching effect. The blander the original, the more amusing the euphemism.
- Onomatopoeia is a great technique for generating memorable slogans ('Slip, slop, slap' for an Australian campaign on the importance of using sunscreen) and product names ('Kerplunk' for, well, Kerplunk).
- If you can successfully turn a name into a generic noun or verb (as in Lazlo Biro's clever pen or W. H. 'Boss' Hoover's vacuum cleaner) then feel free to consider yourself a business writing god.

CHAPTER FOUR

TURNING HEADS

FIGURES THAT MAKE THE ORDINARY EXTRAORDINARY

This chapter focuses on a single main figure of speech – the mighty *chiasmus*. Why the blatant favouritism? Well, the chiasmus is an absolute corker and deserves the widest possible exposure – an opinion not unconnected with the fact that it's my favourite figure. More objectively it's also the magic ingredient that gives many great speeches their greatness and many famous wits their wittiness. After we've gorged ourselves on a feast of chiastic plenty we'll settle our stomachs with the palette-cleansing *hyperbaton* and *antithesis* before downing a couple of petit fours in the form of *anadiplosis* and *parallelism*.

CHIASMUS
SAY WHAT YOU MEAN AND MEAN WHAT YOU SAY

Definition
Chiasmus: *A figure of speech made up of two clauses, the second of which is a reversal of the first.*

Let's start with an old joke: what's the difference between a boxer and someone who has a cold? The answer, of course, is:
'The first one knows his blows, the second blows his nose.'

Sorry about that, but it does give a quick peek into the world of the chiasmus, the 'criss cross' figure responsible for such lexical lovelies as:
'You can take the boy out of Essex, but you can't take Essex out of the boy.'

'When the going gets tough, the tough get going.'

And:
'Judge not, lest ye be judged.'

To get technical for a moment, the chiasmus (the Latinised form of the Greek word for 'crossing') is a figure of speech based on a neat trick called 'inverted parallelism'. All this means is that a chiasmus includes two connected words or phrases that mirror each other in some witty way in order to make a larger point.

US writer Calvin Trillin dubbed the chiasmus a 'reversible raincoat sentence', and you can see what he was getting at. The two-into-one format that all chiasmus share sets up a natural internal dynamic that draws the constituent clauses together, making the resulting phrase appear to mean much more than it says. That's why the chiasmus is so effective – it's a great way of tying up the loose ends of an argument with a neat rhetorical bow.

Such a trim, inviting structure has appealed to the wordies of the world for millennia, imparting as it does instant intellect to what might otherwise be a straightforward sentence. Let's have a few examples.

Mae West, the original good time girl, is also good for two all-time classic chiasmus:

'It's better to be looked over than overlooked.'

And:

'It's not the men in your life that counts, it's the life in your men.'

Incidentally...

Mae's trademark walk was intended to emphasise her femininity yet was copied from female impersonators popular during the marvellously-named 'pansy craze' of the 1920s. For a few brief years gay subculture went overground across America, possibly inspired by the 'anything goes' attitude of the time. Oddly this surprising tolerance disappeared with the end of prohibition. By 1940, anti-obscenity laws were so strict that even the internationally famous female impersonator Julian Eltinge (who'd been a huge star of mainstream stage and screen) couldn't get a waiver from the LAPD to perform in drag. Instead he was forced to wear a tux and glumly point to his gowns hanging on racks behind him.

As well as being an actress, producer and director, Mae was an accomplished writer for the stage and screen, an advocate of gay rights and a victim of censorship throughout her career, even doing time for 'corrupting the morals of youth' (she was sentenced to ten days, but only served eight on the grounds of 'good behaviour' – ironic given her charge). Her wordplay was entirely genuine, with the famous, 'Is that a gun in your pocket' line delivered apparently off-the-cuff to a policeman assigned to protect her.

Ernest Hemingway was particularly fond of the chiasmus, or 'double dicho' as he called it ('dicho' is 'saying' in Spanish). In A.E. Hotchner's biography *Papa Hemingway* he gives this brief explanation of the form's appeal in relation to the novel he was writing at the time, *The Old Man and the Sea* (for which Hemingway subsequently won a Nobel Prize):

'There is at the heart of it [the novel] the oldest double dicho I know.'
'What's a double dicho?' I asked.
'It's a saying that makes a statement forward or backward. Now this dicho is: "Man can be destroyed but not defeated".'
'Man can be defeated but not destroyed.'
'Yes. That's its inversion, but I've always preferred to believe that man is undefeated.'

Apparently Hemingway was fond of asking people which version they preferred: '*Man can be destroyed but not defeated'*, or '*Man can be defeated but not destroyed'*. It's an interesting thought, especially given Hemingway's failing health at the time and his ultimate suicide. Perhaps not surprisingly given this troubled background, another of Hemingway's double dichos was:

'Thought is the enemy of sleep. Sleep is the enemy of thought.'

Another keen coiner of chiasmus was Benjamin Franklin, the man said to have 'invented being struck by lightning' after his famous key-tied-to-a-kite-in-a-thunderstorm experiment. Franklin was a man of many remarkable talents and between 1732 and his death in 1753 wrote and published *Poor Richard's Almanack*, a sort of annual Google-cum-Wikipedia of its time that contained all manner of useful stuff including weather predictions, agricultural ideas, astrological guff, stories, recipes and pithy maxims, several of which took the form of a chiasmus. Here are a few to whet your whistle:

Eat to live, and not live to eat.

Keep thy shop, and thy shop will keep thee.

And famously:

We must all hang together, or assuredly we shall all hang separately.

The *Almanack* was a major success, selling up to 10,000 copies every year. When one of his brothers died, Franklin sent 500 free copies to his widow so she could sell them and avoid penury. Cash would surely have been more help to the grieving woman, but there you go.

Incidentally...

Despite the catty quote about being struck by lightning, Franklin really was a prodigious inventor. Amongst his more remarkable creations were bi-focal glasses, the lightning rod, a snazzy glass musical instrument called an Armonica (not Harmonica) and a remarkably heat-efficient stove that still bears his name. Despite being a canny businessman, Franklin never patented a single invention, saying, 'We should be glad of an opportunity to serve others by any invention of ours; and this we should do freely and generously.'

Winston Churchill, as so often in this book, provides excellent value for money. While strolling down a London street in the company of his infant grandson, Churchill was stopped by an acquaintance who remarked on their similarity. Winston's now-famous response was:

'All babies look like me. But then, I look like all babies.'

Staying with Churchill for a moment, the great man was famous for his prodigious appetite for alcohol, leading to this chiasmic quip to Clement Atlee when censured over his drinking:

'Always remember, Clemmie, that I have taken more out of alcohol than alcohol has taken out of me.'

It seems Winston's taste for the strong stuff has been embroidered over the years, initially by the man himself and later in books like this one. The truth, sadly, is more prosaic. In *My Early Life* Churchill describes how, as a young man in India and South Africa, the water was frequently unfit to drink, necessitating the addition of a little whisky which, 'by dint of careful application I learned to like.' His whisky and water was, according to his wartime private secretary Jock Colville, so weak as to be more akin to mouthwash than a highball. In fact it would appear that his delight in drink was at least partly a prop designed to help bolster the myth of the man. The same was true of his trademark cigars, which were often allowed to go out, rarely smoked beyond a third and usually discarded after being well-chewed.

Incidentally...

There are endless drink-themed stories surrounding Churchill. A personal favourite records that Churchill was invited to speak to an audience of rural bigwigs in deepest middle England. As soon as he finished he called for questions. The first came from a middle-aged woman dressed in hairy tweeds. 'Mr Churchill, I am a member of the Temperance League,' she said, 'My local branch has been examining your use of alcohol. Are you aware Prime Minister that, during your lifetime you have consumed enough alcohol to fill this hall up to here?' stretching her arm dramatically to indicate the picture rail on the wall. 'We want to know what you intend to do about it.' Churchill looked at the woman, followed her arm to the point on the wall, and then slowly allowed his gaze to move up to the ceiling before replying, 'So much to do, so little time.'

Churchill was far from alone in his love for the chiasmus. This figure is much employed by politicians (or more correctly their speechwriters) of every stripe, for the simple reason that the results have an instant states-man-like ring to them. In fact one of the most famous chiasmus of all time is Kennedy's, 'Ask not what your country can do for you...' line. What's less well known is that the speech this comes from, delivered as part of his inaugural address on 20th January 1961, contains a rousing series of chiasmus that expand on each other. Here's the quote in question:

> *'And so, my fellow Americans: ask not what your country can do for you – ask what you can do for your country.*
>
> *My fellow citizens of the world: ask not what America will do for you, but what together we can do for the freedom of man.*
>
> *Finally, whether you are citizens of America or citizens of the world, ask of us the same high standards of strength and sacrifice which we ask of you.'*

Although the full address itself is almost 1,400 words long, it's the 18 words of Kennedy's, 'Ask not...' excerpt that we're still talking and writing about 50 years later, such is the power of a well-worked figure.

Incidentally...

Kennedy created the US Peace Corps in the weeks following his inaugural address, with his 'ask what you can do for your country' line credited with attracting the initial rush of volunteers. Its mission was (and indeed remains) as follows: 'To promote world peace and friendship through a Peace Corps, which shall make available to interested countries and areas men and women of the United States qualified for service abroad and willing to serve, under conditions of hardship if necessary, to help the peoples of such countries and areas in meeting their needs for trained manpower.' Sounds reasonable enough, although that didn't prevent early accusations of spying and colonial imperialism. Since 1960, more than 195,000 people have served as Peace Corps volunteers in 139 countries. President Jimmy Carter said that his mother, who'd served as a nurse in the program, had 'one of the most glorious experiences of her life' in the Peace Corps, although he didn't say what it was.

Not that Kennedy's writers came up with this construction themselves. This particular criss-cross has been doing the rounds on the US speaker circuit for decades. In 1916 Warren G. Harding delighted the Republican Convention with, 'We must have a citizenship less concerned about what the government can do for it and more anxious about what it can do for the nation.' Twelve years earlier a Harvard professor, Le Baron Russell Briggs wrote, 'The youth who loves his Alma Mater will always ask, not "What can she do for me?" but "What can I do for her?"' It's possible the originator of this timeless chiasmus was US Supreme Court judge Oliver Wendell Holmes, who wrote in 1884, 'It is now the moment when by common consent we pause...to recall what our country has done for each of us, and to ask ourselves what we can do for our country in return.'

Of course Kennedy isn't the only politician to invoke the power of the chiasmus. In a speech delivered on St. Patrick's Day 2008 at George Washington University, Hillary Clinton unleashed a classic chiasmus to attack Barack Obama, her then-opponent in the race for the Democratic nomination:

> *'The true test is not the speeches the president delivers; it's if the president delivers on the speeches.'*

It's slightly sad to reflect that although this is a thoroughbred chiasmus, a lack of Classical knowledge coupled with rampant political cynicism means that many of us condemn such super-eloquent rhetorical structures as mere soundbites. Moving on, Barack Obama wasn't exactly adverse to similar tactics and techniques. The very next day he pronounced:

> *'In the end, then, what is called for is nothing more, and nothing less, than what all the world's great religions demand: that we do unto others as we would have them do unto us.'*

Clearly politicians – particularly the US variety – just love the chiasmus. Here are a few more examples, presented in chronological order with Republicans to the right (naturally) and Democrats to the left (hardly):

> *'What counts is not necessarily the size of the dog in the fight – it's the size of the fight in the dog.'*
>
> Dwight D. Eisenhower

'People are more impressed by the power of our example than the example of our power.'
Bill Clinton

'Whether we bring our enemies to justice or bring justice to our enemies, justice will be done.'
George W. Bush

'It is not enough to preach about family values, we must value families.'
Hillary Clinton

'Some people use change to promote their careers; other people use their careers to promote change.'
Sarah Palin

'My job is not to represent Washington to you, but to represent you to Washington.'
Barack Obama

Finally, Mitt Romney, a Republican presidential nominee in 2008, gave us, 'Freedom requires religion, just as religion requires freedom'. Romney's remark doesn't make much sense and raises more questions than it answers, but that's the great thing about the chiasmus – even meaningless nonsense can sound meaningful if criss-crossed correctly.

As with a fair few of the figures we'll examine in this book, the chiasmus has an extremely close cousin – in this case the *antimetabole*. The differences are subtle – too subtle in fact to concern us greatly. Nevertheless, for the record, an antimetabole is the repetition of words in successive clauses, but in

Incidentally...
The chiasmus isn't limited to an exchange of words; it can also involve the exchange of letters or syllables, as in Dorothy Parker's, 'I'd rather have a bottle in front of me than a frontal lobotomy' (artlessly recycled by Tom Waits as, 'I'd rather have a free bottle in front of me than a prefrontal lobotomy' after he noticed the original phrase scrawled on a lavatory wall).

transposed grammatical order, for example, 'I know what I like, and I like what I know'. Other familiar antimetaboles include Bruce Forsyth's trademark, 'Nice to see you, to see you nice', Shakespeare's 'Fair is foul, and foul is fair', Dr Seuss', 'I meant what I said, and I said what I meant. An elephant's faithful, one hundred percent!' and a little more seriously, Winston Churchill's, 'Now this is not the end. It is not even the beginning of the end, but it is, perhaps, the end of the beginning.'

Impressively moustachioed philosopher Friedrich Nietzsche provided a metaphysical antimetabole in the form of:

'Is man one of God's blunders, or God one of man's blunders?'

To which one is tempted to reply, 'Say Fred, you're the philosopher, why don't you tell us?' In a similar vein, Samuel Johnson elegantly (if rather cruelly) put down a young writer keen to know the good Doctor's opinion of his work thus:

'Your manuscript is both good and original; but the part that is good is not original, and the part that is original is not good.'

Incidentally...

All antimetaboles are chiasmi, but not all chiasmi are antimetaboles. That sentence is, of course, itself a chiasmus.

Staying with the antimetabole, Dorothy Parker deliberately implied this figure when she explained a tardy manuscript submission with the line 'too fucking busy, and vice versa.' She was on her honeymoon at the time, so it seems a decent excuse. Similarly, when George Bernard Shaw was contacted by a theatrical producer about the possibility of staging a play the latter had rejected years before, Shaw cabled this implied chiastic reply:

'Better never than late.'

The 'better late than never' idiom this is based on provided the raw material for a series of award-winning press and poster adverts for courier service Fed Ex. These featured a pair of hands unwrapping a package containing an ancient and long-redundant cassette recorder or games console, with the strapline, 'Late is as good as never'. The implication

– that if a package doesn't arrive on time then there's no point in it arriving at all – was underscored by the signoff line, 'Nobody's in a bigger hurry than we are'.

Using much the same technique, one of the many superb print ads for *The Economist* magazine used the line:

'Great minds like a think'

Which neatly inverts the '…think alike' ending we expect the idiom to use. The result attracts our attention twice – the first time because it flips the expected order of the phrase, and the second time because it describes a literal truth – great minds do indeed like a think. Neither the Fed Ex or *Economist* lines are 100 per cent chiasmic in the strict sense of the word, yet both use a criss-cross technique of sorts to achieve their effect. The point is that flipping the elements of a phrase is a quick, easy and highly effective technique for any business writer to include in their toolbox.

Getting back to the antimetabole, this quote from the film *Mystery Men* – concerning a group of utterly useless superheroes – reveals another side to the figure:

Mr Furious: Am I the only one who finds these sayings just a little bit formulaic? "If you want to push something down, you have to pull it up. If you want to go left, you have to go right." It's…

The Sphinx: Your temper is very quick, my friend. But until you learn to master your rage…

Mr Furious: …your rage will become your master? That's what you were going to say. Right? Right?

The Sphinx: …not necessarily.

The Sphinx is addicted to antimetabole for the same reason so many of us are – it lends our words instant gravitas with its pleasing equilibrium and rhythm, although as Mr Furious points out, that doesn't mean you're actually saying anything. Here's another from the same film:

The Sphinx: When you learn to balance a tack hammer on your head, you will head off your foes with a balanced attack.

See what I mean? Nonsense, but good, clean, balanced nonsense with a veneer of profundity.

Lastly, let's lower the tone with an antimetabole from an old *Rocky Horror* radio ad that has Riff Raff threatening, 'If you don't come see this movie, I will belt you around the mouth, and mouth you around the belt.'

Hopefully all this chiastic excess has alerted you to the fact this figure makes marvellous straplines, slogans and other business soundbites. For the business writer interested in crafting a high impact, high recall phrase, the chiasmus is the way to go (which is exactly why political speech writers love it so). Here are a handful of marketing chiasmi to get you going:

'Simply amazing. Amazingly simple.'
Apple iMac

'You like it. It likes you.'
Seven Up

'Live to ride, ride to live.'
Harley Davidson

'The question isn't whether Grape-Nuts are good enough for you, it's whether you're good enough for Grape-Nuts'

'I'm stuck on Band-Aid, and Band-Aid's stuck on me.'

'Friendly Americans win American friends.'
US Travel Service

The criss-cross bit brings the chiasmus to life by presenting a mirror image of a concept for the purposes of persuasion. It rebuts a point by turning it about face. Along the way it makes the commonplace seem compelling, as these business-type examples show:

'We're not too big for the small jobs, or too small for the big jobs.'

'People don't care how much we know until they know how much we care.'

'Management is doing things right, leadership is doing the right things'
Peter Drucker

Remember our implied chiasmus? These too find their way in the world of ads:

'The best lives of our years'
For A&ETV's *Biography* series

'You can tell a lot about a company by the people they keep'
Microsoft

Lastly, and apropos of nothing, I can't resist leaving you with this chiasmus used to describe Alaskan women, who according the US Census Bureau outnumber men in that snowy state by 114 to 100:

'The odds are good, but the goods are odd.'

AND THERE'S MORE
OTHER EXTRAORDINARY FIGURES

So much for the chiasmus and its pal the antimetabole. Another figure that helps turn the everyday into the extraordinary is the *hyperbaton*, an inversion of the normal word order (or alternatively the separation of words which belong together, usually to emphasise the first of the sepa-

> **Definition**
> **Hyperbaton:** *A figure of speech that reverses the normal order of words for emphasis or effect.*

rated words or to create a particular image). So Milton uses this figure in *Paradise Lost* when he writes, 'High on a throne of royal gold...Satan exalted sat,' instead of 'Satan sat exalted...'.

The word 'hyperbaton' is built from two Greek words meaning 'beyond' and 'treading' to give a literal meaning of 'overstepping.' You can clearly see the overstepping in action in Shakespeare's *Comedy of Errors* when Adriana says, 'Why should their liberty than ours be more?' (Act 2, Scene 1). Going back further, Roman rhetorician Quintillion thought hyperbaton a thing of 'positive value', and commented in his *Institutio Oratoria* (a complete survey of rhetoric in 12 books):

'Language would very often be rough, harsh, limp, or disjointed if the words were constrained as their natural order demands and each, as it arises, were tied to the next.'

Quintillion also told a (probably apocryphal) story about the first four words of Plato's greatest work, *The Republic,* which read 'kateben chthes eis Peiraia', and translate as 'Yesterday he went down to the Piraeus...' It seems that after Plato's death his followers were putting his affairs in order and while clearing his room came across clay tablets on which these four words were written out again and again in endless different orders as a series of rough drafts. As Quintillion says, 'He was trying to make order contribute as much as possible to harmony'. That's hyperbaton in a nutshell: it's about mixing up the order of words within a phrase or sentence to make them more effective or vivid.

As you can imagine, it's a figure much loved by poets and lyricists. We've already seen Milton use it to good effect; now consider, if you will, that most catchy of Gilbert & Sullivan tunes (from *The Pirates of Penzance*) 'I am the Very Model of a Modern Major-General'. A series of hyperbatons help make it one of the most amusing in the G&S repertoire:

I am the very model of a modern Major-General
I've information vegetable, animal, and mineral
I know the kings of England, and I quote the fights historical
From Marathon to Waterloo, in order categorical
I'm very well acquainted, too, with matters mathematical
I understand equations, both the simple and quadratical
About binomial theorem I'm teeming with a lot o'news
With many cheerful facts about the square of the hypotenuse.

Anyone with the front to rhyme 'lot o'news' with 'hypotenuse' deserves our admiration.

By now the film fans amongst you might be thinking, 'I'm sure that funny way of speaking sounds familiar'. If so you'd be right, because

Yoda, the *Star Wars* character we last met in the introduction, is a Hyperbaton Master as well as a Jedi Master. Here he is in action:
> *'Sorry I be but go you must.'*

> *'Ready are you? What know you of ready? For eight hundred years have I trained Jedi. My own counsel will I keep on who is to be trained.'*

> *'Named must your fear be before banish it you can.'*

And famously:
> *'Size matters not.'*

There is a surprisingly simple method in Yoda's madness; generally he just takes the first word or few words of a sentence and puts them at the end and – bingo – instant otherwordlyness. Despite being harmless fun Yoda's verbal tick really annoys some people. Anthony Lane, writing in *The New Yorker*, had this to say:
> *'What's with the screwy syntax? Deepest mind in the galaxy, apparently, and you still express yourself like a day-tripper with a dog-eared phrase book. "I hope right you are." Break me a fucking give.'*

Which I rather like (or should that be, 'Like which I rather'?)

Frank Oz, the US film director, actor and puppeteer who voiced Yoda is the chap responsible for his dodgy diction. From a technical perspective, Yoda uses an object-subject-verb word order instead of the more normal English subject-verb-object sequence. In the *Star Wars* universe Yoda's species and home planet are never stated, but here on Earth the object-subject-verb order is downright rare. It crops up in Xavante, a language of the eastern Mato Grosso region of Brazil, as well as in Yiddish and when Sardinians speak Italian. Native English speakers use the object-subject-verb order (if they use it at all) in the future tense or with the conjunction 'but', as in: 'To the pub I shall go!' or 'I hate sprouts, but parsnips I'll eat'. It also appears in relative clauses where the relative pronoun is the object, such as 'What I do is my own business.' Another example is 'With this ring, I thee wed', an example of a phrase that deviates from the standard subject-verb-object sequence but is still universally accepted as real English.

Of course 'real English' is a thorny subject, cluttered as it is with archaic rules that tend to interrupt the flow of meaning. Take, for example, the injunction that you should never end a sentence on a preposition – who cares? Certainly not Winston Churchill, who penned this putdown to a pedantic colleague who insisted on rearranging every sentence that ended on a preposition:

'This is the sort of English up with which I will not put.'

So to sum up, the hyperbaton is about 'inversion to attract attention'. It's this grandstanding tendency that makes it useful to business writers, particularly anyone concerned with making their message stand out.

Definition
Antithesis: *A figure of speech in which sharply contrasting ideas are juxtaposed.*

Another figure that helps make the ordinary extraordinary is the *antithesis*. In our everyday chat, antithesis usually means the opposite or negation of something but the figure of the same name is a subtly different expression of the same idea. An antithesis (Greek for 'setting opposite') is a counter-proposition that means the opposite of the original proposition. The idea is to highlight a contrast in meaning through a contrast in expression. As with so many figures, this definition only really makes sense with the addition of an example, so let's have one:

'That's one small step for man; one giant leap for mankind.'

They are, as if you didn't know, the words of Neil A. Armstrong, spoken as he stepped on to the Moon's surface on 20th July 1969. Armstrong was soon joined by Buzz Aldrin, and the two astronauts proceeded to spend 21 happy hours collecting 46 pounds of moon rock before beginning their lengthy journey home. You've probably heard of those two, but spare a thought for poor Michael Collins – all that training, all that hassle getting there, only to hang around in orbit as 'the other guy'.

It's interesting, although perhaps churlish, to note that the first words spoken by a human being on a heavenly body other than Earth were misspoken. What Armstrong meant to say was:

'That's one small step for "a" man; one giant leap for mankind.'

Analysis of the transmission in 2006 seemed to show that the missing 'a' was masked by static, although the result was far from conclusive. That's not surprising; even the man himself isn't sure what he said. In his 2005 biography Armstrong acknowledged that there doesn't seem to be enough space for the 'a' to slot into the sentence, before going on to say, 'I would hope that history would grant me leeway for dropping the syllable and understand that it was certainly intended, even if it wasn't said – although it might actually have been.' Alas, an even more recent study in 2009 shows that Armstrong couldn't possibly have completed the phrase correctly. An analysis of the original tapes using a voice print spectrograph clearly shows the 'r' in 'for' and 'm' in 'man' running into each other. So no space for the 'a' after all.

Even though he slightly fluffed his big line, Armstrong still crafted a truly brilliant sentence that captured the magnitude of the moment (and better still, he apparently thought of it himself as he struggled into his space suit while still on earth). At the moment of mankind's most remarkable technological achievement, Armstrong turned to a form of words that dates back to the Classical orators of ancient Greece and Rome, which only underscores how powerful and appealing figures of speech can be.

Interestingly...

There's a glorious urban myth told about Neil Armstrong which suggests that immediately after the famous line about mankind he mutters the following strange words: 'This one's for you, Jablonski.' When questioned about its meaning Armstrong replied, 'I grew up in Ohio. Mr Jablonski lived next door, and one night I heard his wife shout: "Oral sex! You want oral sex! You'll get oral sex on the day that the kid next door walks on the Moon." I just wanted to tell him the good news.' It's a lovely story but unfortunately it's utterly untrue.

Let's have some more antitheses to bring us back down to earth:
Action, not words.

To err is human, to forgive, divine.

Many are called, but few are chosen.

And indeed:
It feels so right it can't be wrong.

All of them use opposites or strongly contrasting ideas placed in sharp contrast or juxtaposition to draw attention to a point, as does this extended example from one of literature's greatest novelists:
'It was the best of times, it was the worst of times, it was the age of wisdom, it was the age of foolishness, it was the epoch of belief, it was the epoch of incredulity, it was the season of Light, it was the season of Darkness, it was the spring of hope, it was the winter of despair, we had everything before us, we had nothing before us, we were all going direct to Heaven, we were all going direct the other way.'
A Tale of Two Cities, Charles Dickens

Here Dickens uses seven successive antitheses to repeatedly highlight the contrasting fortunes of different groups in the years immediately prior to the French Revolution. Remarkably, *A Tale of Two Cities* has sold over 200 million copies and is the most printed original book written in English (just ahead of *Scouting for Boys* By Baden-Powell and Tolkien's *The Lord of The Rings*.)

Moving on, the *anadiplosis*, from the Greek for 'doubling back' is the repetition of the last word of a preceding clause. The word is used at the end of one sentence and then used again at the beginning of the next, for example:
'In the beginning God made the heavens and the earth. The earth was without form and void, and darkness was upon the face of the deep.'
Genesis 1:1-2

Or:

> *'The land of my fathers. My fathers can have it.'*
> Dylan Thomas on Wales

One of the good things about the anadiplosis is that they can be chained together to create a sort of rhetorical rollercoaster that just builds and builds. It's a rousing technique much loved by those seeking to make a point:

> *'Aboard my ship, excellent performance is standard. Standard performance is sub-standard. Sub-standard performance is not permitted to exist.'*
> Queeg in Herman Wouk's *The Caine Mutiny*

And:

> *'The general who became a slave. The slave who became a gladiator. The gladiator who defied an emperor. Striking story.'*
> Commodus in the movie *Gladiator*

> *'Once you change your philosophy, you change your thought pattern. Once you change your thought pattern, you change your attitude. Once you change your attitude, it changes your behaviour pattern and then you go on into some action.'*
> Malcolm X

You may also recall Yoda's anadiplosis ('Fear leads to anger...') at the very start of this book. Any figure of speech used by Yoda, Malcolm X, Dylan Thomas and God is all right by me.

Parallelism is a figure that comes in forms various (see what I did there with the hyperbaton?) The two main ones we'll cover are the *isocolon* and the *tricolon*, both close enough to pure-bred parallelism to render their differences irrelevant. As I've said before, the edges of these categories are often a bit smudged, making it hard to know for sure where a particular example belongs, so don't let it worry you. In fact forget I ever said it.

Parallelism – in all its forms – is about giving two or more parts of a sentence a similar shape so as to give the whole a well-defined form. It yields phrases like Caesar's:

'I came, I saw, I conquered.'

Or on a larger scale, JFK's:

'Let every nation know, whether it wishes us well or ill, that we shall pay any price, bear any burden, meet any hardship, support any friend, oppose any foe to assure the survival and the success of liberty.'

These examples show that parallelism can work at the word, phrase or clause level, making it a practically flexible figure. In fact, once you start looking, this structure turns up everywhere:

'Government of the people, by the people, for the people.'
Abraham Lincoln

'When you are right you cannot be too radical; when you are wrong, you cannot be too conservative.'
 Martin Luther King, Jr

'I don't want to live on in my work. I want to live on in my apartment.'
Woody Allen

In all three of these examples the writer gives his utterance rhythm and bounce by repeating certain parts – in Lincoln's case it's 'the people', in King's it's 'when you are' and 'you cannot be too', and in Allen's it's 'want to live on in my'. Once the audience gets the hang of what's happening they start subconsciously anticipating the next instalment, which gently draws them in and encourages them to keep listening.

The great thing about parallelism is that it imparts instant erudition:

'It is by logic we prove, but by intuition we discover.'
 Leonardo da Vinci

'Never in the history of mankind have so many owed so much to so few.'
Winston Churchill

'The louder he talked of his honour, the faster we counted our spoons.'
Ralph Waldo Emerson

'Climate is what we expect, weather is what we get.'
Mark Twain

It's this quality that makes parallelism a gift to ad writers. Try these for size:
'It takes a licking, but it keeps on ticking.'
Timex watches

'Everything you want, nothing you don't.'
Nissan automobiles

'The closer you get, the better you look.'
Nice 'n' Easy Shampoo

'I'm a Pepper, he's a Pepper, she's a Pepper, we're a Pepper, wouldn't you like to be a Pepper, too?'
Dr Pepper

Admittedly the last example is bordering on plain ol' repetition, but it's parallel repletion, and that's the point. And while we're on the subject, this example of a business writer repeating himself may amuse. It appeared on a card insert in a magazine encouraging people to subscribe. The insert included the usual yes/no tick boxes, beside the first of which was the expected line:
Yes! I want a one-year subscription

But instead of following with a 'no' version, the second line read:
Yes! I want a one-year subscription

Naturally the magazine was called *Positive Thinking*.

Most of the above examples come vaguely under the heading of *isocolon*, from the Greek for 'of equal members or clauses', which basically means they tend to be in two halves. Next I'd like to introduce the *tricolon* which, as its names suggests, involves three members or clauses. It's the same parallel structure but in three parts:

'Tell me and I forget. Teach me and I remember. Involve me and I learn.'
Benjamin Franklin (again)

'Be sincere, be brief, be seated.'
Franklin D. Roosevelt's excellent advice to public speakers

'The key to taking Springfield has always been Elm Street. The Greeks knew it. The Carthaginians knew it. Now you know it.'
'Bart the General', *The Simpsons*

'I think we've all arrived at a very special place. Spiritually, ecumenically, grammatically.'
Captain Jack Sparrow in *Pirates of the Caribbean*

Like the isocolon, the tricolon is a figure much loved by those in the persuasion business:

'Eye it, try it, buy it.'
Chevrolet slogan

'Admire, Aspire, Acquire'
Flag on the Victoria Quarter Arcade, Leeds

And before you write off these last two examples as the crass marketing nonsense they so clearly are, remember that they're driven by the same dynamic that made 'Veni, vidi, vici' such a hit. Like any figure, it all depends how you use it.

One particularly effective example of the tricolon in action comes courtesy of a recent magazine ad for Honda cars. The text ran thus:

There is a place where dreamers go. Where crazy flights of fancy are valued above all else. Where the only good idea is an idea that's never been had before. Where dreams can become real. It's called The Patent Office, Concept House, Newport, just off the M4, Junction 28, first roundabout, fourth exit.'

Before ending with the strapline:

Honda: the power of dreams.

Without wishing to analyse the magic out of this nifty paragraph, the three sentences beginning with 'where' create an increasing sense of expectation and excitement, which is then amusingly dashed by the Concept House comedown. It's a build 'em up/knock 'em down thing, and very effective it is too.

This sort of parallelism is one of the most useable figures in business writing – you don't have to be a great orator or wit to make this one work, all you need is to spot the possibility of presenting the points of your argument in a neat, equivalent way. Parallelism comes into its own when you're comparing related items or writing anything vaguely list-like, for example:

Our IT services range from design and installation to support and maintenance.

Here the sentence uses an intuitive 'from…to' structure supported by parallel 'X and Y' clauses (for example 'design and installation'). Or this:

In the coming year we face serious challenges related to increasing component costs, changes to demand and aggressive overseas competitors.

Here each of the three 'challenge' points is three words long and begins with an adjective, making them pleasingly parallel.

If you're writing instructions then parallelism has an equally important role. The main point to make here is that each step in the instruction sequence must begin with a verb (that's what an instruction is):

How to bring business language to life:
1. *Read Roger's book*
2. *Do everything he says*
3. *Make everyone you know buy a copy*

All these examples of parallelism introduce a rhythm to the writing that's both attractive and practical. By making the structure of your sentences predictable (in the best possible way) you'll help your readers make sense of them. The trick, as I say, is to use grammatically equivalent structures presented in a regular, reliable format. Try to keep your sentences approximately the same length and use the same tense and tone of voice. With a little imagination you can use parallelism to present a complex group of ideas in a way that doesn't read like a list:

Although the proposed design of our new website is visually appealing, it doesn't address key points in the brief. Although relatively easy to produce, it won't be cost effective in the long term. Although technically innovative, it won't be easy to maintain.

Here the parallel form (combined, as you may have noticed, with three big dollops of antithesis) draws attention to the contrasting points in the argument and helps create a paragraph that's both musical and informative. And that's what bringing business language to life is all about.

IN A NUTSHELL
TOP TIPS FOR BUSINESS WRITERS
- In need of instant profundity? Then do what generations of political speechwriters have done and try mirroring one part of your phrase to create a pithy rejoinder. This technique is also a brilliant way of

generating put downs and witty comebacks during spirited verbal jousts.

- Try flipping elements of common idioms to coin catchy phrases or straplines. Try using opposites or contradictions to draw attention to or affirm your point.
- Parallelism is a gift to business writers. If you've got several related things to say, try finding a nice, regular structure in which to say them. You can present the results in either sentence form or as bullets.
- Remember what we might call 'the rule of two' (isocolon) and 'the rule of three' (tricolon) – both are readymade structures ripe for exploitation and specific examples of parallelism in action. In all these cases try to keep your clauses around the same length and structured in the same way (otherwise they won't be parallel).

CHAPTER FIVE

TICKLING YOUR READER'S FANCY

FIGURES OF FUN

It's not all sober stuff when it comes to figures of speech. Several are dedicated to nothing more serious than raising a smile. Of course, this being the realm of rhetoric we're talking wordplay and witty repartee rather than guffaw-laden gags (well, for the most part). The first figure we'll meet is the *pun*, raw material of any number of advertising headlines and memorable bon mots. After that we'll encounter the sadly underused *zeugma* (my number two fave figure of all time, after the chiasmus), followed by *spoonerisms* and *malapropisms*. These last two are essentially comic, but that doesn't mean they can't pull their weight in the world of work.

PUN
GONE CHOPIN, BACH IN A MINUET

Definition

Pun: *A playful substitution of words that are alike in sound but different in meaning. For example James Joyce's 'As different as York and Leeds' instead of 'chalk and cheese'.*

It's been said that 'to pun is to treat homonyms as synonyms'. Hmm, accurate but opaque. More helpfully we could say that a pun involves the deliberate confusion of words or phrases that look or sound alike for humorous or thought-provoking effect. So a pun, strictly speaking, is nothing more than a second meaning that works by exploiting either an assumed equivalence between similar words or the different shades of meaning attached to a single word.

Let's have some examples. In *Alice's Adventures in Wonderland*, Lewis Carroll writes:

'And how many hours a day did you do lessons?' said Alice, in a hurry to change the subject.

'Ten hours the first day,' said the Mock Turtle, 'nine the next, and so on.'

'What a curious plan!' exclaimed Alice.

'That's the reason they're called lessons,' the Gryphon remarked: 'because they lessen from day to day.'

Shakespeare's *Richard III* includes this famous poetic pun:

'Now is the winter of our discontent made glorious summer by this son of York'

Act 1, Scene 1

Based, I hardly need point out, on the similarity of 'son' and 'sun'. Even Jesus couldn't resist the urge to pun, as this beauty from Matthew 16:18 makes clear:

'Thou art Peter, and upon this rock I will build my church.'

Here the pun relies on the fact that in Greek the word 'rock' (petra) is close to the name 'Peter' (petros) which – conveniently – also means 'stone'.

Finally, let me just mention that the cod-medical term 'funny bone' – the popular name for the sensitive exposed nerve located where the humerus joins the ulna at the elbow – derives its name from a pun on 'humerus' and 'humorous'. Crazy guys, those anatomists.

The word 'pun' has been in use since at least 1550, although the origins of the word itself are obscure. Over the last 500 years many writers and commentators have written and commentated on this most contentious of figures. Jonathan Swift claimed that, 'Punning is an art of harmonious jingling upon words, which, passing in at the ears, excites a titillary motion

Incidentally...

Puns can be visual as well as verbal. The artist and engraver Hogarth once sent out a dinner invitation which pictured a knife, a fork, and a pie with three Greek letters: eta, beta, pi. Likewise ace graphic designer Paul Rand once playfully reworked IBM's logo as a picture of an eye, another of a bee, and then a final letter M. Strictly speaking such a visual pun or word puzzle is called a rebus.

'non-profit institution'. Then there are *compound* puns (as in the apocryphal sign in a golf-cart shop which reads, 'When drinking, don't drive. Don't even putt') and *extended* puns (such as the distinctly fishy, 'I don't want to carp on, but if we flounder about and perch on the fence we'll be all over the plaice').

Another punning format is the *Tom Swifty*, a phrase in which a quoted sentence is linked by a pun to the way it's delivered. So for example,

Incidentally...
Tom's exploits and inventions have inspired many great minds over the years, including science fiction giant Issac Asimov and Steve Wozniak, co-founder of Apple Computers. Numerous gadgets, including policemen's favourite, the taser, are said to have been inspired by Tom's fictional creations.

'"Pass me the shellfish", said Tom crabbily', or '"I used to be a pilot", Tom explained' (ex*plain*-ed – geddit??). The name comes from a series of books written for teenagers between 1910 and (amazingly) 2007 in which the young scientist hero, Tom Swift, gets into improbable adventures involving rocket ships and ray-guns and other cool stuff he's invented.

A *daffynition* is a rather obscure form of pun that involves the reinterpretation of an existing word on the basis that it sounds like another word or group of words, for example: 'Alarms: What an octopus is' (alarms/all arms – ahem*)* or 'Pasteurise: Too far to see' (pasteurise/past your eyes – oh never mind). Similarly, a *transpositional pun* involves swapping the words in a well-known phrase or saying to get a daffynition-like redefinition of a well-known word unrelated to the original phrase, such as 'Hangover: The wrath of grapes' or 'Dieting: the waist is a terrible thing to mind'.

Moving on, a *feghoot* is a pun used as the punchline to a rambling story or shaggy dog tale. This snippet comes from the 2003 movie *Master and Commander: The Far Side of the World*, although the feghoot Aubrey uses is many years older:

Captain Aubrey (who has enjoyed several glasses of wine): Do you see those two weevils, Doctor? Which would you choose?
Dr Maturin: Neither. There's not a scrap of difference between them. They're the same species of...Curculio.

Captain Aubrey: If you had to choose. If you were forced to make a choice. If there were no other option.

Dr Maturin: Well then, if you're going to push me. I would choose the right-hand weevil. It has significant advantage in both length and breadth.

Captain Aubrey: There! I have you! You're completely dished. Do you not know that in the Service, one must always choose the lesser of two weevils?

Lastly, let us look briefly at *knock-knock* jokes, all of which are driven by puns. Although popular in places as diverse as Belgium, South Africa and India, not to mention the UK, these so-called jokes are unknown in other countries including Brazil and Germany. Obviously they don't always begin 'knock-knock' – in French they begin 'Toc-Toc', in Afrikaans and Dutch it's 'Klop-klop', while in Spanish the format changes so that the punchline rhymes with the response. Shakespeare's *Macbeth* even includes a sort of extended knock-knock gag in Act three, Scene three with a character – Porter – using this format to drunkenly welcome sinners to hell. Well, it loses something in the describing.

How does all this help the business writer eager to express himself with more eloquence? Well, as I mentioned at the top of this chapter, puns make marvellous slogans and headlines. By adding a dash of humour they attract readers' attention and help get through the mental defences all readers construct to deal with marketing message overload. Puns are also popular with writers themselves for the simple reason that they're fun to create and offer the opportunity to spice up an otherwise straight-faced piece of business communication. These examples show you what I mean:

'When it rains, it pours.'
Morton Salt

'When it pours, it reigns.'
Michelin tires

'Every bubble's passed its fizzical.'
Corona soft drinks

'Our sages know their onions.'
The Times newspaper

'Coke refreshes you like no other can.'
Coca-Cola

'Ask for More'
More cigarettes

And staying with the 'more' theme, SSL International, makers of Durex, chose to advertise their new 'climax delay' condoms with a slogan spelt out in condom-shaped lettering that cheekily emphasised the key benefit of their new product:
'Roger more'

In my other life as a copywriter I once wrote a series of lines for a sewage treatment company that punned merrily on the theme of, ahem, shit:
We deal with **it.
Leave **it to us.
**it happens.
Do **it right.
We love **it.

And so on. These *Carry On*-style lines proved highly effective. In fact they're the best proof I can offer that this whole figures of speech in business writing thing works. The campaign in question doubled the client's turnover in 12 months without any additional marketing spend and was directly responsible for grabbing this small company the lead story of *The Times* business section. Not bad for a few dodgy puns.

Finally, no section on punny business writing would be complete without some mention of *The Economist* magazine and their long running (and quite superb) print advertising campaign. Almost entirely text-based, it has included such masterful pun-based lines as:

'Free enterprise with every copy'

'Attracts magnates'

'Honing device'

and

'Utter brilliance'

Brilliance indeed. What makes these so special is their (no pun intended) economy – the pun format allows the writer to pack far more into the phrase than would otherwise be possible; the result is some of the best business writing created anywhere. No wonder crafting one of these legendary lines is considered the pinnacle of many an advertising copywriter's career.

All these examples avoid slipping into cheesy territory. However, one category of business writing that gleefully – one might say *wantonly* – embraces the pun's potential for cheese is shop names. The nation, and no doubt the world, is awash with such 100 per cent genuine inanity as:

The Codfather (fish & chip shop)

Alexander the Grate (fireplace showroom)

Curl Up and Dye (beauty salon)

The Lone Hydrangea (florist)

Womb to Grow (maternity wear)

All Cisterns Go (plumbing service)

Barber Blacksheep (hair salon)

Cycloanalysts (bicycle shop)

Napoleon Boiler Parts (heating supplies)

Junk & Disorderly (furniture store)

Get Stuffed (taxidermist)

Sew Fantastic (haberdashers, right next door to Get Stuffed on Islington's Essex Road)

SOMETHING FOR THE WEEKEND, SIR?

What all these names – cheesy and non-cheesy – have in common is what we might call 'bidirectionalism'. No, wait, come back – like the 'bistable illusion' we met earlier, 'bidirectionalism' means these puns work both ways, in other words, they make sense (sort of) no matter how you read them. *That's* the hallmark of a good business pun: all the various readings somehow coexist peaceably with the same few words. So when John Deere Tractors use the slogan:

'Nothing runs like a Deere'

...we get it, no matter how we choose to read It (a tractor that runs well or a particularly fleet-footed mammal). Likewise, Kellogg's *All Bran* breakfast cereal advertised itself by emblazoning the sides of its distribution lorries with the huge slogan:

'Trouble passing?'

This not-so-subtle but vaguely amusing line draws attention to the positive effect All Bran's high levels of roughage can have on digestive regularity, while punning on the difficulty a motorist may have overtaking the enormous articulated lorry carrying said cereal. I'm the first to admit this technique doesn't produce great literature, but it certainly works.

Sadly this bidirectionalism sometimes goes wrong. Over the years the manufacturers of various soft-top cars have used (and indeed reused) the slogan, 'To air is human'. That's fine when you read it straight – feeling the wind in your hair as you drive can indeed be one of life's little pleasures – but the other reading – 'to err is human' – doesn't make sense in this context and in fact casts a shadow over proceedings by implying that driving with the top down (or even buying that particular car) is somehow a mistake, albeit one any human could make. The lesson for business writers is clear – puns have power, but they need to be used wisely to ensure they don't backfire.

OK, to summarise: all puns are driven by ambiguity, in the case of business puns this tends to focus on interpreting an item both as part of an idiom and a lexical item in its own right. The classic example is the slogan, 'Players please', which works both as a request and as a statement regarding the satisfaction that a particular brand of cigarette delivers. By actively promoting this ambiguity (what a linguist would call 'homonymy'), business writers can introduce some humour into their work and provoke interest in their words.

Incidentally...

Ideas of what counts as pun-based wit clearly vary from place to place. It's unlikely the New South Wales anti-litter campaign that rejoiced under the headline 'Don't be a tosser' would succeed in Surrey.

Before we leave puns we may find it instructive to pause briefly on a closely related figure, the *antanaclasis* (from the Greek meaning 'reflection' or 'bending back'). This close cousin of the pun involves repeating a single word but with a different meaning each time. Like other kinds of pun, the antanaclasis is often found in slogans, hence its relevance for business writers:

If you don't look good, we don't look good
Vidal Sassoon

People on the go, go for Coke
Coca-Cola

Cats like Felix like Felix
Felix cat food

Computers help people help people
IBM

If you don't get it, you don't get it
The Washington Post slogan

The long cigarette that's long on flavour
Pall Mall cigarettes

You get the idea. The antanaclasis also makes for a witty repost, as in Churchill's, 'Your argument is sound...all sound', Vince Lombardi's, 'If you aren't fired with enthusiasm, you'll be fired, with enthusiasm', and US president Calvin Coolidge's, 'The business of America is business.'

Finally, I leave you with proof that figures of speech can prove shockingly promiscuous as a chiasmus shacks up with an antanaclasis to form this phrase (courtesy of Ambrose Bierce):

'The gambling known as business looks with austere disfavour on the business known as gambling'.

ZEUGMA
DISCONTINUE USE IF YOU FEEL PAIN OR FAINT

Here's a word you don't meet every day. A zeugma (from the Greek for 'yoke') is a figure of speech in which a verb or an adjective is applied to two or more nouns when its sense only really applies to one of them (or possibly both but in different ways). Take the example, 'She aroused men and suspicion' – here

> **Definition**
>
> **Zeugma:** *A word that modifies or governs two or more other words when it's appropriate to just one of them. For example, 'The farmers grew broccoli and bored'.*

'aroused' is the zeugma as it yokes together 'men' and 'suspicion'. The Rev Henry Peacham, father of all things figure-ish and hero of this book, praised the zeugma as a 'delight to the ear' although he cautioned against using 'too many clauses', for reasons that will hopefully become clear.

Very closely related to the zeugma are the *syllepsis* (Greek for 'a taking together') and the *ellipsis* (from the Greek for 'to fall short') – so closely related in fact that we'll treat them all as one. The dictionary says that in a syllepsis the various clauses, which are often in the form of a pun, don't necessarily make sense. For this reason it's sometimes said that a syllepsis is a union of incongruous elements, which accounts for its popularity in comic or satiric situations. However, that description is equally true of the zeugma proper, so once again a so-called definition fails miserably to do its job. Just stick with the idea that zeugma, syllepsis and ellipsis all do very much the same thing and you won't go far wrong.

By now you might be thinking, that's all very well but who on earth uses such an obscure construction? The answer is 'plenty of people', for the pleasing reason that the zeugma is rather less obscure and rather more useful than it might appear at first blush.

An example or two feels in order. Shakespeare (naturally) comes up trumps with this beauty from the final line of Sonnet 128:

> *'Give them thy fingers, me thy lips to kiss.'*

Then Canadian songstress Alanis Morissette sang:

> *'You held your breath and the door for me.'*

Where, yep, you guessed it, 'held' is the zeugma.
Then there's this, courtesy of Hawkeye from *M*A*S*H*:
'*Are you getting fit or having one?*'

Incidentally...
The phrase 'smart alec' apparently arose from the exploits of Alec Hoag, a celebrated pimp, thief and confidence trickster operating in New York during the 1840s.

Which is exactly the sort of smart alec one-liner you'd expect from him. Let's have some more. Stephen Fry provides us with the following somewhat smug zeugma, spoken around the time of his finals at Cambridge:
'*All my friends are getting Firsts and married.*'

While Dickens contributes this from *Pickwick Papers*:
'*Miss Bolo...went home in a flood of tears and a sedan chair.*'

Mark Twain gave us 'covered in dust and glory' in *The Adventures of Tom Sawyer*, and Groucho Marx proffered the marvellous:
'*You can leave in a taxi. If you can't get a taxi, you can leave in a huff. If that's too soon, you can leave in a minute and a huff.*'

Never one at a loss for words, Oscar Wilde included the following in *The Importance of Being Earnest*:
'*Oh, flowers are as common here, Miss Fairfax, as people are in London.*'

This is particularly clever because the speaker, Cecily, is making a catty remark to Miss Fairfax, a Londoner, by using 'common' in the senses of both 'numerous' and 'vulgar'.
Lastly, and in stark contrast, Uncle Fester of the *Addams Family* once admitted:
'*I live in shame and the suburbs.*'

Enough – I think we're all clear that a zeugma is a sort of two-for-the-price-of-one construction. Now let's go deeper. The world of figures is rarely straightforward, so it shouldn't come as any surprise to find that the plain old zeugma also exists in several more exotic guises. I absolutely acknowledge that at this point you may be straining to catch the sound of hairs being split, but these sub-figures are definitely worth investigating, if only so that you can justify using their outrageously spelt names during a closely-fought game of Scrabble.

A *prozeugma* (otherwise known as a *synezeugmenon* – no, really) involves a verb followed by one or more yoked nouns, for example, 'I speak sense, you nonsense' or 'I ran to the store; Steve to the station; Anna to the rescue.' Without using a prozeugma we'd have to rewrite this as: 'I ran to the store; Steve ran to the station; Anna ran to the rescue'. No one would lose their job over the lengthier version but the prozeugma version is just that bit more elegant, and that's what we're after. Here's another predictably fluid example from Dickens:

> *'He proposed seven times; once in a hackney-coach, once in a boat, once in a pew, once on a donkey at Tunbridge Wells and the rest on his knees.'*
> *Little Dorrit*

The *mesozeugma* involves using a verb in the middle of a sentence to govern several parallel clauses on either side of the verb, as in this example from Cicero: 'Both determination and virtue will prevail; both dedication and honour, diligence and commitment'. Here 'prevail' is the mesozeugma.

In a *diazeugma* a noun is modified by one or more subsequent verbs without being repeated, for example: 'Lucy woke up, leapt out of bed and got dressed'. Without a trusty diazeugma to hand the sentence would read: 'Lucy woke up, Lucy leapt out of bed and Lucy got dressed' – distinctly lumpy.

Finally, the *hypozeugma*. Unlike the zeugmas described above, here the yoking word *follows* the words it connects. For example, 'Hours, days, weeks, months and years seemed to slip away'. Without the hypozeugma this would read, 'Hours seemed to slip away, days seemed to slip away, weeks seemed to slip away...' well, you get the point. One of the more famous examples of the hypozeugma (also called an *adjunctio* in Latin) is Shakespeare's 'Friends, Romans, Countrymen, lend me your ears.' A hypozeugma-less version would read, 'Friends, lend me your ears; Romans, lend me your ears; Countrymen, lend me your ears', and that would never do.

A really great example of the hypozeugma is the unofficial motto of the US Postal Service:

'Neither snow nor rain nor heat nor gloom of night stays these couriers from the swift completion of their appointed rounds.'

This lovely line is a translation of words written in the fifth century BC by Herodotus, the Greek writer known as 'the father of history' and is included in his masterwork *On the Persian Wars*. In it, Herodotus praises the stamina and persistence of mounted messengers in the service of Xerxes, King of Persia. In fact it seems Herodotus borrowed the construction from a similar formulaic phrase that appears in Homer's *Odyssey*, probably first written down three or four hundred years earlier.

Incidentally...

The United States Postal Service has no official motto. However, the 'Neither rain, nor sleet, nor...' line is carved onto the façade of the James Farely Post Office in New York, hence the confusion. Despite its unofficial status the USPS used this line as part of a TV ad following the anthrax postal scares of 2001, such is its popular appeal. Interestingly, these are also the words that Norm from the TV show Cheers *mistakenly gets tattooed on his buttocks after a drinking session with postman Cliffe goes horribly wrong. They also form part of Laurie Anderson's rather wonderful 1981 hit* O Superman.

Let's leave this hypozeugmatic confusion with a final example, courtesy of Mr Burns from *The Simpsons*:

'Family, religion, friendship. These are the three demons you must slay if you wish to succeed in business.'

Zeugmas matter to business writers for two reasons. Firstly they're beautiful, economical and memorable in their own right. And secondly they help us express the relationship between ideas and actions with remarkable clarity and distil our message into something both punchy and palatable. You can imagine zeugmatic business phrases like:

'OK team, get your laptops and into the conference room.'

'Neither he nor we are going to sign that contract.'

And indeed:

'The best salesman gets a pat on the back and a £1,000 bonus.'

True, using a zeugma at work won't be a daily occurrence, but that's almost the whole point. Good business writing takes the occasional risk so be brave and, when the occasion demands, really let rip. In that situation a zeugma could be just what you need.

Finally, by way of a conclusion I must share with you this zeugmatic overload from gentle 1950s comic duo Flanders and Swann, taken from their song *Madeira M'Dear*.

He had slyly enveigled her up to his flat
To view his collection of stamps
*And he said as **he hastened to put out the cat,***
The wine, his cigar and the lamps:
"Have some Madeira, m'Dear!
You really have nothing to fear."

Unaware of the wiles of the snake in the grass
And the fate of the maiden who topes,
She lowered her standards by raising her glass,
Her courage, her eyes and his hopes.

She let go her glass with a shrill little cry.
Crash! Tinkle! It fell to the floor.
*When he asked "What in Heaven?" **she made no reply,***
Up her mind, and a dash for the door.

Lovely stuff.

SPOONERISM
'THREE CHEERS FOR OUR QUEER OLD DEAN!'

Definition

Spoonersim: *The involuntary transposition of sounds in two or more words, for example 'scoop of boy trouts' for 'troop of Boy Scouts'.*

A spoonerism is a play on words in which corresponding consonants, vowels, or morphemes (bits of words) are moved around for comic effect, usually by mistake. At a more sophisticated level spoonerisms function as a form of pun and can be used deliberately to achieve rhetorical results, hence their place here. Deliberate or otherwise, spoonerisms all work the same way: the sounds that are reversed usually come from the beginnings of the words and often from the syllable that carries the stress, for example:

It is kisstomary to cuss the bride

Spoonerisms are named after the Reverend William Archibald Spooner (1844–1930), Warden of New College, Oxford. Rev Spooner had distinct word-tangling tendencies, although nothing like as much as legend would have us believe. He was aware of his reputation and thoroughly disliked it. On one occasion, after the concept of spoonerisms became wildly popular, Spooner denounced a crowd that had gathered to hear him speak with the words, 'You haven't come for my lecture, you just want to hear one of those...*things.*'

Most of the quotations attributed to Spooner are apocryphal. In fact *The Oxford Dictionary of Quotations* lists only one genuine, substantiated spoonerism uttered by the man himself: 'The weight of rages will press hard upon the employer' (he meant to say something about 'the rate of wages'). Which is rather odd, as Spooner himself claimed that 'The Kinquering Congs Their Titles Take' (in reference to a hymn, and instead of 'Conquering Kings...'), was his sole spoonerism.

Either way, most so-called spoonerisms were made up by Rev Spooner's colleagues and students as a sort of genial, intellectual hobby. As Michael Quinion reports, this seems to have been motivated by fondness rather than malice, as Spooner himself (affectionately known as the Spoo) was kindly and well-liked. Today the Middle Common Room of New

College, Oxford is informally known as 'The Rooner Spoom' in Spooner's honour.

Having debunked the myth of Spooner's mix-ups let me now attempt to reinstate it, at least partially. Spooner *did* transpose things, but not in the way his reputation would suggest. For example, a reliable witness reports him repeatedly referring to a friend of a Dr Child as 'Dr Friend's child'. In fact, Spooner was prone to all manner of absent-minded gaffs. On one occasion he invited a fellow don to tea, 'to welcome Stanley Casson, our new archaeology Fellow'. 'But, sir,' the man replied, 'I *am* Stanley Casson'. 'Never mind,' Spooner said, 'Come all the same.' At a party his wife sustained a cut on her finger. When concerned friends asked him, 'Did she lose her finger permanently?' he is alleged to have answered, 'She lost her finger permanently, for a time.' One recorded incident had Spooner write a note asking for a fellow lecturer at New College to see him immediately about a vital matter. The note had a postscript informing the recipient that the matter had been resolved and he no longer needed to see him. A strange and lovely man.

Incidentally...

'Spoonerism' is just the latest name for this particular linguistic phenomenon. In a previous life it was known as a 'Marrowsky', after a Polish count of that name who suffered from the same impediment. The earliest attestation of Marousky (spellings vary, believe me) is in 1863: 'Fanny King', or as Bill Leach, in the interesting language called Marousky, termed her, 'Kanny Fing'.

Why am I bothering you with the oratorical shortcomings of a long dead professor? Because old Spoo's errors strike a chord in many of us. It seems we're all somehow predisposed to spoonerise, usually for fun but sometimes unconsciously. Ever said 'flutterby' for butterfly? Or 'par cark'? Of course you have. While it might be too much to say we're hardwired that way, we're certainly partial to playing with language in a Spooner-ish manner.

Popular examples of spoonerisms include one of Kenny Everett's more popular characters, a blonde woman named 'Cupid Stunt' (bizarrely the original name of 'Mary Hinge' was rejected as too risqué), while comedian Jasper Carrott claims to have an aunt who frequently makes spooner-isms, referring to him as a 'shining wit'.

More modern day examples include a British newsreader referring to a 'hypodeemic nerdle'; a television announcer saying that, 'All the world was thrilled by the marriage of the Duck and Doochess of Windsor' and that news regarding an impending presidential veto had come from 'a high White Horse souse' (instead of 'White House source'). Although these aren't true spoonerisms, these days any syllable exchange seems to fall under that heading.

Of course it's not just Spooner who spooned. Peter Sellers in the *Pink Panther* sequel *A Shot in the Dark* gave us the pleasing, 'killed him in a rit of fealous jage', while in the Mel Brooks movie *Robin Hood: Men in Tights*, the Sheriff of Rottingham utters such phrases as 'He deered to kill a King's dare.' In an episode of *The Simpsons* when Sideshow Bob tries to murder Bart (again), Chief Wiggum barks at his men, 'Bake him away, toys!' Finally, and closer to home, Ronnie Barker uttered the following immortal spoonerism in *Open All Hours*, 'Don't just crit there siticising.'

MALAPROPISM
'IT'S NOT THE HEAT, IT'S THE HUMILITY'

Definition

Malapropism: *The tendency to confuse words that are similar in sound, often for comic effect. For example Dan Quayle's remark that 'Republicans understand the importance of bondage between a mother and child.'*

Like the last lexical curiosity we encountered – the spoonerism – a malapropism isn't exactly a figure of speech in the sense of having grown out of the demands of Classic rhetoric. Both are more recent, more amusing inventions. The other thing they have in common – and let me be honest here – is that it's pushing things slightly to say either has a major contribution to make to business writing. But that's not the point – with these two figures (and indeed many others) what I aim to do is open your eyes and ears to the possibilities in language, and make a heartfelt plea to be just a bit braver when it comes to using words at work. You won't often get the opportunity to spoonerise or malapropise between the hours of nine and five, but think how much impact your words will have when you do. These sections are about interest and inspiration rather than everyday techniques. Believe me, it all adds up.

Anyway, malapropisms. If you're not familiar with the word you'll certainly know the construction it describes – the swapping of one word for another similar sounding one, usually for comedic purposes. So in the classic britcom *Steptoe and Son*, Harold exclaims, 'What are you incinerating?', while Tigger in *Winnie the Pooh* asks himself, 'Where are my mannerisms?'. 'Insinuating' and 'manners' are, of course, what they meant to say.

The word 'malapropism' comes from a character – Mrs Malaprop – in Richard Sheridan's 1775 play *The Rivals*. As you can probably imagine, the good lady is prone to mixing up her words, for example, 'He is the very pine-apple of politeness!' (instead of 'pinnacle') and, 'He will dissolve my mystery!' (instead of 'resolve').

The act of word mixing for laughs is altogether older. The word *mala-propos*, meaning 'inappropriate' or 'inappropriately', comes from the French phrase *mal à propos* (literally 'ill-suited'). The earliest English use of malapropos in the sense we're interested in dates from 1630 – 145 years before Sheridan's dramatic doings. Going back even further, Shakespeare's *Much Ado About Nothing* (1598) includes a character called Dogberry – a bumbling police officer of sorts – who malapropises with abandon:

'You are thought here to be the most senseless and fit man for the constable of the watch'
Act 3, Scene 3
where 'senseless' should be 'sensible'.

'Our watch, Sir, have deed comprehended two auspicious persons'
Act 3, Scene 5
where 'comprehend' should be 'apprehend' and 'auspicious' should be 'suspicious'.

And:
'O villain! Thou wilt be condemned into everlasting redemption for this'
Act 4, Scene 2

where 'redemption' should be 'perdition'. How they must have rolled in those Elizabethan aisles.

Incidentally...
Dogberry is a sort of Ur-character for any number of hapless law enforcement operatives, including Sheriff Buford T. Justice (Smoky and the Bandit), Sheriff Rosco P. Coltrane (The Dukes of Hazard), Inspector Clouseau (The Pink Panther) and Sheriff J.W. Pepper (Live and Let Die and The Man With the Golden Gun).

Today we're equally keen on malapropisms and for just the same reason: humour. A consistently reliable source is *The Sopranos*, where one character memorably describes himself as 'prostate with grief'. In another episode Tony Soprano says, 'I've got these two albacores around my neck' and characterises an event as 'creating a little dysentery among the ranks.'

If you think you see a pattern emerging you'd be right. For a malapropism to earn its stripes it must sound similar to the word it stands in for. Using *obtuse* (wide or dull) instead of *acute* (narrow or sharp) is not a malapropism; using *obtuse* (stupid or slow-witted) when one means *abstruse* (esoteric or difficult to understand) most certainly would be. Likewise, simply making up a word, or adding a redundant or ungrammatical prefix (*irregardless* instead of *regardless*) or suffix (*subliminible* instead of *subliminal*) to an existing word won't cut it as a malapropism. To make the point let's have some more genuine examples.

'I want to be effluent mum!'

'You are effluent Kimi...'

Kath and Kim, where 'effluent' should of course be 'affluent'.

'It just seems awfully mean. But sometimes, the end justifies the mean.'
The Office

'Let's talk about a very tattoo subject.'
Da Ali G Show, where 'tattoo' should be 'taboo'. Elsewhere Mr G refers to *'BLT'* instead of *'WMD'*.

'It's good to be back on the old terracotta'
Del Boy in *Only Fools and Horses*, who presumably meant to say 'terra firma'.

Finally, *New Scientist* recently reported the first-ever malapropism for 'malapropism', when, having become aware of his error, an office worker apologised, saying he had committed a 'Miss Marple-ism.'

All good stuff, and great for lightening the mood in any piece you might be writing. But we cannot leave this carnival of confusion without a nod and a wink towards three major malapropisers: George W. Bush (responsible for a strain of malapropisms known as 'Bushisms'), sports commentator David Coleman (coiner of Colemanballs), and US baseball legend Lawrence Peter 'Yogi' Berra (the man behind Yogi-isms).

First Dubbya, complete with the date and place his words were uttered to prove I'm not making this up:

'Rarely is the questioned asked: Is our children learning?'
Florence, S.C., 11ᵗʰ January 2000

'They misunderestimated me.'
Bentonville, Ark., 6ᵗʰ November 2000

'You teach a child to read, and he or her will be able to pass a literacy test.'
Townsend, Tennessee, 21ˢᵗ February 2001

'Our enemies are innovative and resourceful, and so are we. They never stop thinking about new ways to harm our country and our people, and neither do we.'
Washington, D.C., 5ᵗʰ August 2004

Next, Colemanballs. The name itself was neologised by the good people of *Private Eye* magazine to describe the mis-sayings of all UK sports commentators, not just the eponymous Mr Coleman. Try these, all malapropisms of a sort:

'Do my eyes deceive me, or is Senna's Lotus sounding rough?'

'That's cricket, Harry, you get these sorts of things in boxing.'

'Here they come, every colour of the rainbow: black, white, brown.'

A recurring Colemanball (and indeed general offence against language) involves the word 'literally', as in, 'He missed the goal by literally a million miles'. Inserting 'literally' changes the 'million miles' bit from a figurative sketch to an apparently factual description, and that's where it all goes wrong.

Finally, Yogi-isms. We mentioned Mr Berra in Chapter 2, but here we can focus on his more malapropistic efforts (such as the 'heat/humility' example at the top of this section.

'He hits from both sides of the plate. He's amphibious.'

'You can observe a lot by watching.'

And the plain barmy:

'I'm not going to buy my kids an encyclopaedia. Let them walk to school like I did.'

There are dozens of these but, like spoonerisms, many were made up by admirers. As the great Yogi himself said, 'I didn't really say everything I said.'

To round off this section, allow me to introduce *mondegreens*, a related phenomenon to the malapropism that describes something being mis-heard rather than mis-said. Song lyrics are a rich source, such as, '*The girl with colitis goes by*' instead of '*The girl with kaleidoscope eyes*.' Another oft-quoted example comes from Jimi Hendrix's *Purple Haze*, mistaking "*Scuse me while I kiss this guy*' for the real lyric of "*Scuse me while I kiss the sky*.' Just to make things interesting, Hendrix deliberately mis-sang this at least once as "*Scuse me while I kiss that guy*'. The result is clearly audible on a live disk included in the 2001 CD *Voodoo Child: The*

Hendrix Collection, although sadly the sleeve doesn't say where or when it was recorded.

The term *mondegreen* was coined by author Sylvia Wright. As a child, Wright heard the lyrics of *The Bonny Earl of Murray* (a lilting Scottish ballad) as:

Ye highlands and ye lowlands
Oh where hae you been?
Thou hae slay the Earl of Murray
And Lady Mondegreen

It eventually transpired that Lady Mondegreen existed only in Wright's mind as the actual lyric reads '...*slay the Earl of Murray and laid him on the green*.' Never mind – Lady Mondegreen is now alive and well in all hard-to-decipher lyrics.

IN A NUTSHELL
TOP TIPS FOR BUSINESS WRITERS

- Never underestimate the power of humour to attract and retain readers' attention – it's a woefully underused weapon in the business writer's arsenal. Keep it witty rather than pant wetting.
- That said, humour that misses the mark is just an embarrassment. Set your bar exorbitantly high. If in doubt seek second opinions.
- Puns can make great headlines/straplines/whatevers *but only if they help make the message more persuasive or memorable*. If you're sure a pun is the way to go, the basic technique is to find your key word, locate another that sounds alike, and swap.
- Try 'folding back' part of a phrase by repeating a single word but with a different meaning to create something memorable (the old 'The business of America is business' shtick).

CHAPTER SIX

SOUNDING SMART

FIGURES THAT ENTERTAIN YOUR EARS

Ah, the drums and music of magical words – we neglect them at our peril. Far from being just a pleasant by-product of message making, the sounds we choose to use have a direct impact on the efficacy of our argument. They make it palatable, memorable and eloquent. As you'd expect, a whole group of figures – sometimes called figures of sound – are here to help. In this chapter we'll start with the best known example of the genre, *alliteration*, before moving on to the publicity-shy *anaphora* followed by *assonance*, *dissonance*, *euphony* and *resonance*. You may be unfamiliar with the names of these figures, but be assured you're already *au fait* with the effect they produce.

ALLITERATION
HOW MUCH WOOD COULD A WOODCHUCK CHUCK IF A WOODCHUCK COULD CHUCK WOOD?

Definition

Alliteration: *The repetition of the beginning sounds of words, such as 'long-lived', 'short shrift' or 'the fickle finger of fate.'*

Alliteration is a stylistic figure in which successive words – or more correctly stressed syllables – begin with the same letter or consonant sound. The word itself comes from the Latin for 'putting letters together' and was coined by a chap called Giovanni Pontano in 1519. It's one of the few figures of speech taught at school and is part and parcel of everyday language, cropping up in common idioms and phrases like, well, 'part and parcel'. News headlines, business names, literary titles, advertising slogans and nursery rhymes all make liberal use of this figure. Thanks to its ability to make the commonplace catchy, alliteration is also at the heart of many a marvellous mnemonic. It's also ideal for any writing aimed at children as the resulting rhythm is a ready-made way of capturing the interest of young readers.

Incidentally...

According to über search engine Wolfram Alpha the answer to the question posed in the subheading above is 'A woodchuck would chuck all the wood he could chuck if a woodchuck could chuck wood'. The scholarly paper 'The Ability of Woodchucks to Chuck Cellulose Fibers' by P.A. Paskevich and T.B. Shea in Annals of Improbable Research vol. 1, concluded that a woodchuck can chuck 361.9237001 cubic centimetres of wood per day.

Let's kick off with some examples – 'it takes two to tango', 'the more the merrier' and 'Peter Piper picked a peck of pickled peppers'. You can see (and of course hear) the matching first letters at work. Like many of our figures, alliteration is much employed by political speechwriters, for example JFK's, 'Let us go forth to lead the land we love', uttered during his inaugural Presidential Address. Likewise, Julius Caesar reached for alliteration when he proudly proclaimed 'Veni, vidi, vici', although as we saw in Chapter 4, once translated his remark loses its alliteration and becomes an example of parallelism. Such is the way with figures – as we progress deeper into their heart of darkness we'll see more and more examples of duplication and boundary crossing.

Incidentally...

A peck is a unit of volume for dry goods equivalent to 16 dry pints. Spookily, two pecks make a kenning, although not the figure we discussed in Chapter 1. Four pecks make a bushel, while four lippies or forpets make a peck. The peck is more or less redundant in the UK, although still occasionally used in the US. A peck of pickled peppers is actually a pretty impressive pile.

As the title of this chapter implies, one of the reasons alliteration is so popular is that it's so pleasing. It makes our words roll in a most delightful way yet requires little effort. Try this double example, from the movie *O Brother, Where Art Thou?*:

Rivers: Hello. Who's the honcho around here?

Head Honcho: I am. Who're you?

Rivers: Well, sir, I'm Jordan Rivers. And these here are the Soggy Bottom Boys out of Cottonelia, Mississippi – songs of salvation to salve the soul.

Or this, spoken by the Wizard of Oz himself:
'Step forward, Tin Man. You dare to come to me for a heart, do you?
You clinking, clanking, clattering collection of caliginous junk. And you,
Scarecrow, have the effrontery to ask for a brain! You billowing bale of
bovine fodder!'

Or this, from Charles Dickens' *Little Dorrit*:
'"Father" is rather vulgar, my dear. The word "Papa", besides, gives a
pretty form to the lips. "Papa", "potatoes", "poultry", "prunes", and
"prism", are all very good words for the lips: especially "prunes" and
"prism"'.

Alliteration was also a big thing in the naming of pre-conquest English
kings. In the ninth century we had an unbroken line made up of Æthelwulf,
Æthelbald, Æthelberht, and Æthelred. These were followed in the 10th
century by their direct descendants Æthelstan and Æthelred II. Later still
the saints (and siblings) Tancred, Torhtred and Tova provide a similar
example. Why the Saxons went in for royal alliteration with such gusto is
unclear, although it may have contributed to a sense of dynastic
continuity.

Poets are attracted to alliteration as a way of increasing the music of a
particular passage. Gerard Manley Hopkins, much-troubled Jesuit
wannabe and inventor of the phrase 'dark night of the soul' made it an
integral part of his 'sprung rhythm'. Here's a snippet, from his poem *Pied
Beauty*, written in 1877 although not published until 1918:
Glory be to God for dappled things...
Landscapes plotted and pieced—fold, fallow and plough;
And all trades, their gear and tackle and trim.

In his masterwork, *The Windhover*, (also 1877/1918) Hopkins alliterates
again:
I caught this morning morning's minion, king-
dom of daylight's dauphin, dapple-dawn-drawn Falcon, in his riding
Of the rolling level

Likewise, Milton gave us, 'Behemoth, biggest born of earth', Shake-speare, 'Full fathom five thy father lies' and Wilfred Owen, 'The stuttering rifles' rapid rattle'. In *The Highwayman* (a poem my septuagenarian mother can still recite in full having learned it at primary school) Alfred Noyes described the moon as 'a ghostly galleon tossed upon cloudy seas' and says 'the road is a ribbon of moonlight over the purple moor'. Alaric Alexander Watts even wrote a full poem – *The Siege of Belgrade* – composed entirely of alliterative phrases, one for each letter of the alphabet:

An Austrian army, awfully arrayed,
Boldly by battery besieged Belgrade.
Cossack commanders cannonading come,
Dealing destruction's devastating doom.

And so on to *'Zeus', Zarpater's, Zoroaster's Zeal'*. Even in the context of the previous 25 lines it makes no sense at all.

You get the point. Poets like alliteration because it's, well, poetic. Another group drawn to this device is advertising copywriters, a group whose job it is to rent mental space in the minds of their readers. For them the attraction is the ease of recall alliteration provides, as this selection of slogans drawn from both sides of the Atlantic makes clear:

Beanz Meanz Heinz

Guinness is good for you

The quicker picker upper

Crispety, crunchety, peanut-buttery Butterfinger

Salon secret for thicker, fuller hair

What we want is Watneys.

Why not waste a wild weekend at Westmore Water Park?

The daily diary of the American dream

You'll never put a better bit of butter on your knife.

In each case the aim is the same: somehow balance the need to distil the message to the bare bones while still making it instantly memorable and – ideally – lovable.

In contrast to many of the figures we've examined, alliteration comes naturally (left to my own devices I alliterate for England, as you may have noticed) and is perhaps the most accessible figure described in this book. Yet this commendable urge to add melody to our words comes with an important caveat: although it looks simple enough, alliteration has to be deliberate to work well. Let it occur naturally and the result can be messy and unrefined. A distinctly shrewish 1939 study by behavioural psychologist B.F. Skinner looked at the alliteration of 's' sounds in 100 Shakespearian sonnets, and concluded that the Bard 'might as well have drawn his words out of a hat', such was the random nature of his alliteration. Regardless of how wrong we might feel B.F. to have been, his larger point is sound: if you alliterate it's important to keep everything under control. Use alliteration by all means, but use it well and for a reason.

At this point it's only fair to point out that not all commentators are keen on this figure. Some condemn it as a lazy, clumsy device used as the headline of last resort by over-caffeinated sub editors, yielding as it does such overwrought headlines as:

Pompey Pipped at the Post as Pippo Pounces

And

Kurdish Control of Kirkuk Creates a Powder Keg

Alliteration comes in for particular criticism from those in the sporting community as a way of creating with sluggish, frequently inappropriate nicknames for rising stars (and indeed the downright obscure). The formula is simple enough: take something personal or geographical and just add something alliterative that may or may not be relevant. Result?

The Dark Destroyer or the Flying Finn. Hearing Muhammad Ali, his speech destroyed by Parkinson's Disease, struggling to describe his pride at lighting the Olympic Flame in Atlanta served as a cruel and poignant reminder of his days as the Louisville Lip.

Alliteration even has a place in the murky world of UK parliamentary politics. It seems that recently many of our MPs have been found contributing a few words to obscure debates several times a day for no other reason than to get their name in the record and win reputations as hard workers worth every penny of their miserly pay. Similarly, many are tabling endless parliamentary questions (usually in Westminster Hall, a sort of third division debating chamber shunned by most MPs) with little interest or regard for the result. It's all about being seen to be busy, as even the briefest utterance in official debate counts as contributing to a speech. To highlight and mock this farcical practice the excellent website theyworkforyou.com has started listing the number of times every MP uses a three word alliterative phrase in debate and how the honourable members rank against each other. UK readers may wish to see how their own MP checks out against this most moronic metric.

Incidentally...

On the subject of names, alliteration has given us Clark Kent, Lois Lane and Lex Luther, Big Ben, the World Wide Web and Coca-Cola, not to mention Donald Duck, Mickey Mouse, Bob the Builder and Spongebob Squarepants – which illustrates my point about alliteration working well for kids.

Enough of that nonsense. Regardless of what the naysayers say, alliteration is the raw ingredient of much humour, as this snippet from Monty Python's *The Life of Brian* shows:

Pilate: *Who is this Wodger to whom you wefer?*

Man1: *He's a wobber.*

Crowd: *Ahhhhahahah.*

Man2: *And a wapist.*

Crowd: *Ahahahhahah!*

Woman: *And a pickpocket!*

Crowd: *Aaah no. Ssssssh.*

It's also what gives tongue-twisters their twist. They typically employ two or three sequences of sounds, then the same sequences of sounds with some sounds exchanged. For example, *She sells sea shells on the sea shore. The shells that she sells are sea shells I'm sure*. There are exceptions, mainly those that rely on repeat-

Incidentally...

If I had a penny for every time some wag followed my first name with the 'he's a wobber' line I'd have a hell of a lot of loose change.

ing a short phrase as fast as possible, such as 'toy boat', 'Greek grapes' or 'big whip' – try saying them as fast as possible and you'll see how unexpectedly tripsome these three are (in the case of 'big whip' it's to do with the dif- ficult lip movement needed to get from the 'g' to the 'wh' sounds). It may interest you to know that according to Guinness World Records, the toughest tongue twister in the English language is supposedly, *The sixth sick sheikh's sixth sheep's sick*.

Incidentally...

The children's book Fox in Socks, *by Dr Seuss, consists almost entirely of densely rhyming, alliterative tongue twisters. And have you noticed that the phrase 'tongue- twister' is itself alliterative?*

Last but not least (see what I did there?), the sign language equivalent of a tongue twister is called a *finger fumbler*. Apparently the phrase 'Good blood, bad blood' is both a tongue twister in English and a finger-fumbler in sign language.

ANAPHORA

Definition

Anaphora: *The repetition of a word or phrase at the beginning of several sentences or clauses, as in this passage from Ecclesiastes 3:1-2 'A time to be born, and a time to die; a time to plant, and a time to pluck up what is planted.'*

LET'S GO ROUND AGAIN. AND AGAIN.

The next figure of sound we'll look at is the shy and retiring anaphora (Greek for 'carrying back') – the repetition of a word or phrase at the beginning of successive phrases, clauses or lines. You're probably not familiar with the figure itself, but you'll certainly know the effect it creates. For example:

'We shall not flag or fail. We shall go on to the end. We shall fight in France, we shall fight on the seas and oceans, we shall fight with growing confidence and growing strength in the air, *we shall defend our island, whatever the cost may be, we shall fight on the beaches, we shall fight on the landing grounds, we shall fight in the fields and in the streets, we shall fight in the hills. We shall never surrender.'*

Sir Winston Churchill, 4ᵗʰ June 1940

This Churchillian chunk is full of anaphora in the form of the repeated, 'We shall' phrase – eleven in total. His 'We shall fight...' speech is often misquoted to include the line 'we shall fight them in the streets', but as you can see he didn't quite put it like that. Rather ironically, given the threat at the time, the really famous part beginning 'We shall fight on the beaches...' and ending '...we shall never surrender', is made up entirely of words with a clear Germanic root (coming to us via Old English), while the only French-derived word is 'surrender'. Churchill almost certainly did this deliberately – the Gallic equivalents of Old English words are always longer and as he once famously remarked, 'little words move men'.

Incidentally...
The early summer of 1940 was of course a critical point for the UK in the Second World War. Churchill rose to the occasion with three major speeches. All have entered the popular imagination – 'Blood, toil, tears, and sweat' on 13ᵗʰ May (his maiden speech in the House of Commons as Prime Minister), 'We shall fight on the beaches' on 4ᵗʰ June, and 'This was their finest hour' on 18ᵗʰ June. Not a bad month's work.

Churchill – brilliant rhetorician that he was – took his cue from an earlier, equally rousing example of anaphora. You'll no doubt recognise this:

'This royal throne of kings, this sceptred isle,
This earth of majesty, this seat of Mars,
This other Eden, demi-paradise,
This fortress built by Nature for herself
Against infection and the hand of war,
This happy breed of men, this little world,
This precious stone set in the silver sea,
Which serves it in the office of a wall,
Or as [a] moat defensive to a house,
Against the envy of less happier lands;

This blessed plot, this earth, this realm, this England,
This nurse, this teeming womb of royal kings,
This land of such dear souls, this dear dear land,
Dear for her reputation through the world,
Is now leas'd out — I die pronouncing it —
Like to a tenement or pelting farm.'

It is, of course, John of Gaunt's big moment in Shakespeare's *Richard II*. As elsewhere, the anaphora ('This') drives home the subject of the speech by covering it from every angle. The repetition creates a sense of momentum that carries all before it, producing a rousing rhythm that cynics might call manipulative, although I prefer to think of it as inspiring. For the hard-pressed business writer, anaphora can be the key to instant public speaking excellence.

If you *do* find yourself reaching for this figure then just remember that modesty can be as important as confidence. The last thing you want is for your reader to think you're saying the same thing over and over again because (a) you haven't got anything else to say and (b) you like the sound of your own voice. As always, the way to bore your audience is to repeat yourself carelessly, excessively, needlessly and endlessly; the way to keep your readers interested is to repeat yourself imaginatively, forcefully, thoughtfully and amusingly. Easier said than done but that's the trick of it.

So in the right hands (or should that be mouth?) the anaphora – and indeed repetition in general – can work wonders. It allows the reader or listener to get involved by subconsciously predicting the next phrase. It invites us to participate and become part of the piece ourselves. Then, when the rhythm is finally broken, we get the delight of surprise and take pleasure in the moment's emphasis. A great example is Dr Martin Luther King, Jr's seminal, 'I have a dream' speech in which he uses the phrase, 'I have a dream that one day...' three times, before the knockout punch of 'I have a dream *today*'. Brilliant stuff.

Unsurprisingly, given its power, the anaphora has found favour with politicians. Many begin their sentences with 'and' while they think of their next point (or remember their script). This gives continuity and flow to their speech, although overusing this device tends to make them sound like mad Old Testament prophets. That wasn't a problem, however, for Franklin Delano Roosevelt who used the anaphora in his Pearl Harbour Address to convey the onslaught America had just suffered:

'Yesterday, the Japanese government also launched an attack against Malaya. Last night, Japanese forces attacked Hong Kong. Last night, Japanese forces attacked Guam. Last night, Japanese forces attacked the Philippine Islands. Last night, the Japanese attacked Wake Island. And this morning, the Japanese attacked Midway Island.'

Likewise Hillary Clinton had this to say at the 1996 Democratic National Convention address:

'To raise a happy, healthy, and hopeful child, it takes a family; it takes teachers; it takes clergy; it takes business people; it takes community leaders; it takes those who protect our health and safety. It takes all of us.'

While Obama caught the mood of the nation with his Audacity of Hope speech on 27th July 2004:

'It's the hope of slaves sitting around a fire singing freedom songs; the hope of immigrants setting out for distant shores; the hope of a young naval lieutenant bravely patrolling the Mekong Delta; the hope of a mill-worker's son who dares to defy the odds; the hope of a skinny kid with a funny name who believes that America has a place for him, too. Hope – hope in the face of difficulty. Hope in the face of uncertainty. The audacity of hope!'

It's enough to make you stand up and salute, which is precisely the point.

Needless to say, it's not all straight-faced, political stuff. The anaphora can be used for comedic purposes, as Homer Simpson makes clear:

'I want to shake off the dust of this one-horse town. I want to explore the world. I want to watch TV in a different time zone. I want to visit strange, exotic malls. I'm sick of eating hoagies! I want a grinder, a sub,

a foot-long hero! I want to LIVE, Marge! Won't you let me live? Won't you...please?'

While this next example, from Monty Python, builds on the aforementioned biblical shtick of '*And* the earth was without form...*and* the spirit of God moved upon the face of the waters, *and* God said, let there be light, *and* there was light...':

Friar: And Saint Attila raised the hand grenade up on high, saying, "O Lord, bless this Thy hand grenade that with it Thou mayest blow Thine enemies to tiny bits, in Thy mercy." And the Lord did grin and the people did feast upon the lambs and sloths and carp and anchovies and orangutans and breakfast cereals, and fruit bats and large chu—

Brother Maynard: Skip a bit, brother

Friar: And the Lord spake, saying, "First shalt thou take out the Holy Pin..."'

The Bible is big on anaphora. Think of Jesus' 'Blessed are the...' sermon on the mount routine (also parodied by the Pythons in their 'blessed are the cheesemakers' redux).

From the sublime to the ridiculous. Advertising is always on the lookout for techniques to increase the impact of its messages, and the anaphora certainly fits that description. Exhibit A, a jingle from the 1950s:

Brylcreem, a little dab'll do ya,
Brylcreem, you'll look so debonair!
Brylcreem, the gals'll all pursue ya!
They'll love to run their fingers through your hair.

Then there's this unintentionally comic masterpiece:
The miracle of VHS. The miracle of JVC technology.

And indeed this for a Proctor and Gamble painkiller:
All day strong, all day long.

Before we take our leave of the anaphora let me just mention a closely related, but mirror image figure, the *epistrophe* (Greek for 'return'). This is the exact counterpart of anaphora, repeating as it does words at the *end* of a clause. It gives us such gems as Abe Lincoln's, 'Government of the people, by the people, for the people' and 'When I was a child, I spoke as a child, I understood as a child, I thought as a child' from 1 Corinthians 13:11. It also underpins American writer and intellectual Gertrude Stein's somewhat unsatisfying philosophy on life:

'There ain't any answer, just you believe me, there ain't any answer... *there ain't going to be any answer, there never has been any answer,* *that's the answer.'*

AND THERE'S MORE

Staying with our theme of figures that deal with the sound of language let's meet *assonance*, the juxtaposition of the same (or similar) vowel sounds with different end consonants. It's sometimes known as a 'vowel rhyme', as in the matching 'ee' sound in the phrase 'sweet dreams', or the subtle 'i' sound in 'hit or miss'.

Definition

Assonance: *A resemblance of vowel sound, as in the phrase* *'tilting at windmills'.*

Assonance is one of the building blocks of verse, although the eponymous student of Willy Russell's *Educating Rita* derided it as, 'getting the rhyme wrong'. Was she right? You decide:

'That solitude which suits abstruser musings'
Samuel Taylor Coleridge

'Season of mists and mellow fruitfulness'
John Keats

'That dolphin-torn, that gong-tormented sea'
W.B. Yeats

Or indeed:
> *'So the FCC won't let me be or let me be me so let me see, they try to*
> *shut me down on MTV but it feels so empty without me'*
> Eminem in his song *Without Me*

I think it works a treat. Staying with hip-hop for a moment, it seems stressed assonance has become a big thing. Early rappers tended to rhyme the *end* of the lines in an almost nursery rhyme fashion:
> *I don't mean to brag, I don't mean to boast,*
> *But we like hot butter on our breakfast toast*

From The Sugarhill Gang's epoch-making *Rapper's Delight*. And this from Slick Rick:
> *Once upon a time not long ago*
> *When people wore pyjamas and lived life slow*

Starting in the 1990s rappers started to get more complex, introducing assonance vowel rhymes into the middle of sentences, as this from Eminem shows:
> *His palms are sweaty, knees weak, arms are heavy*
> *There's vomit on his sweater already, mom's spaghetti*

And this assonant (and alliterative) couplet from 2Pac:
> *Niggaz be actin' like they savage, they out to get the cabbage*
> *I got nuthin' but love for my niggaz livin' lavish*

Incidentally...

Figures often crop up in the same sentence – the phrase 'paper has more patience than people' from The Diary of Anne Frank *contains a metaphor, alliteration and assonance in just six words.*

The point is that assonance – like alliteration – helps direct attention towards particular words, nudging the reader to make an association they might otherwise miss. Careful use of alliteration and assonance can also help establish rhythm or make an existing rhythm more complex by influencing which words are naturally stressed. So although they're superficially similar, assonance has a subtler effect than alliteration, and often operates at a semi-subconscious level. It's one of the things that helps us decide whether a particular pair of words sound good together, as in this slogan for Avis Car Rental:

I hate to wait

What's more, we can group vowel sounds into high and low groups, depending on where our tongue is in our mouth as we're speaking. For instance, 'i' in 'dish' is high, whilst 'u' in 'pub' is low. In fact grouping lots of high or low vowel sounds together is the basic technique of assonance. Most native English speakers subconsciously associate high vowels with light, elegant or sophisticated things, and low vowels with the cruder stuff of everyday life, for no other reason than that's the way they've been used historically in our language. Clearly you can take advantage of this to establish the tone of a piece of writing – if you want spirits raised and moods lightened just reach for the 'eye' and 'eee' sounds.

The flip side of assonance – or vowel rhyme – is *consonance* – or consonant rhyme, as in 'riff raff' or 'pitter patter'. It's different to alliteration in that alliteration requires the repeated consonant sound to be at the *beginning* of each word, while in consonance the repeated sounds can occur anywhere within the word, although it's often at the end. Still on a hip-hop tip, here's an example from the song *Zealot* by The Fuggees:

Rap rejects my tape deck, ejects projectile/Whether Jew or gentile I rank top percentile.

And another, this time from *Do Not Go Gentle Into That Good Night* by Dylan Thomas:

'Curse, bless, me now with your fierce tears, I pray'

Closely related to assonance and consonance are our final three figures in this chapter: *dissonance*, *euphony* and *resonance*. What's special about these three is the range over which they work. Alliteration, assonance and consonance all achieve their effect by focusing on the sounds of individual letters and how those sounds create rhythm and rhyme.

Incidentally...
A special species of consonance involves using a series of sibilant sounds. Several examples of sibilance occur in Edgar Allan Poe's poem The Raven. *For example: 'And the silken sad uncertain rustling of each purple curtain' – note the additional assonance based on the 'ur' sound. Sibilance works a treat because some sounds carry particular cultural associations. If you're familiar with* The Lord of the Rings, *think how Gollum's extra 's' sounds make him seem creepy and untrustworthy.*

However, dissonance, euphony and resonance all demand a slightly enlarged view and require us to look at a piece of speech or writing *as a whole* in order to achieve their effect. For this reason their impact on a piece's overall tone and feel can be considerable.

Definition

Dissonance: *a deliberately harsh, disagreeable combination of word sounds.*

Euphony: *the opposite of dissonance; a pleasant sounding or harmonious combination of words.*

Resonance: *the intensification of particular word sounds for poetic or musical effect.*

Let's have some definitions. Dissonance, or cacophony, is the mixing or bringing together of harsh, discordant sounds that are somehow grating to the ear. For example, Churchill's:

'We want no parlay with you and your grisly gang who work your wicked will.'

What counts as harsh or discordant can be pretty subjective, although this line, by the poet Carl Sandburg, is often cited as an example:

Poetry is the synthesis of hyacinths and biscuits.

Here Sandburg uses clashing, abrasive sounds to create dissonance which in turn accentuates the almost surreal choice of words (a similar approach was taken by the band Nurse with Wound for the title of their first LP, *Chance Meeting on a Dissecting Table of a Sewing Machine and an Umbrella*). The effect is to emphasise how poetry can bring together, and somehow reconcile, ideas and elements that have no natural affinity.

At the opposite end of the scale is *euphony*. This refers to the harmony or beauty of a sound that creates a pleasing effect on the ear. It's achieved not only by the choice of particular words, but also by their relationship in the sound patterns of a piece. As I mentioned earlier, euphony is more a product of an extended passage than a short segment.

So, how do you start euphonising? Well, vowels tend to have a more pleasing sound than consonants, and vowels that require a rounded mouth when pronounced (typically u and o) yield the most musical sounds. But we can go further: consonants with a liquid sound (such as m, n and r) add to euphony, whereas clipped sounds (like k, p and t) tend to create a staccato feel. Likewise, explosive sounds (for example b, t and v) can detract from euphony and cause you to veer, like a drunk driver trying to text his mates at 60mph, into the roadside ditch of dissonance.

Lastly but not leastly in this section on sound let's look at *resonance*. Here we're really pushing the definition of figures of speech to its limit, as these techniques all emphasise sound over meaning, although in practice the two can rarely be fully separated. Resonance is related to euphony in that it aims to create a pleasing, restful feel. The difference is that resonance does this by using repetition to create a smooth, comforting rhythm. It all starts with word choice. To get some resonance into your speech or writing you need to choose words that end in prolonged sounds – for example, the word 'hum' has the potential for a long, drawn-out ending that lingers on the 'm' sound. Classic resonance letters include l, m, n and r, along with the prolonged, breathy sounds of f and v and the sibilant sounds of s and sh. Here's an example from W.B. Yeats' *The Lake Isle of Innisfree*:

I will arise and go now, and go to Innisfree,
And a small cabin build there, of clay and wattles made;
Nine bean-rows will I have there, a hive for the honey-bee,
And live alone in the bee-loud glade.

I won't deny that these last few figures of sound find their natural home in poetry rather than business writing, but that doesn't mean they can't be repurposed for prose. In Hart Crane's poem *The Bridge* (1930), he uses cacophony to communicate the chaos and evil in the industrial world:

The nasal whine of power whips a new universe,

Where spouting pillars spoor the evening sky

There's no reason whatsoever why such turns of phrase shouldn't appear in your work, in fact I positively encourage it. Business writers have much to learn from those working in other disciplines, poets in particular. There are plenty of parallels between business writing and poetry, not least that poetry is about using as few words as possible to say as much as possible – economy, power and recall are all common concerns. And let's not forget that poetry is a great way to sensitise yourself to language, a superb source of phrases for the creative business writer to steal and above all else food for the soul. I commend it to you.

IN A NUTSHELL
TOP TIPS FOR BUSINESS WRITERS

- Alliteration is an effortless way to make the commonplace catchy and create high-recall phrases out of the most unpromising source material. It works equally well for highlighting headings or when submerged within sentences.
- If you choose to alliterate, do it deliberately and with confidence. If the effect seems random then it detracts from your credibility. Equally, don't overdo it – nothing cloys like too many clashing consonants.
- Repetition of a word or phrase at the beginning (or end) of successive phrases, clauses or lines is a technique much exploited by dramatists and speechwriters to increase the intensity of a passage. Business writers can use the same method to achieve the same effect.
- Think about the *sound* of your words. Assonance, dissonance, euphony and resonance can direct attention to a particular word or phrase, establish a rhythm in your writing and influence the entire mood of a piece.

CHAPTER SEVEN

WORDS THAT CAN WOUND

FIGURES TO PROVOKE, MOCK OR CONFUSE

As we approach the end of this book it's time to put aside all thoughts of consensus, conciliation and agreement, and unleash a group of figures whose function is to vex, ire and rile. Actually, that's a bit strong – the three figures we'll cover here – *oxymoron*, *irony* and *sarcasm* – are consummately creative and have far more about them than is often supposed. Sure, they make for outstanding insults, but they also give us scope to exercise our intelligence and express ourselves in a way that goes straight to the heart of the situation. Although all three are outwardly familiar you might be surprised to find what lies beneath.

OXYMORON
A FIGURE OF MODEST MAGNIFICENCE

An oxymoron (plural 'oxymora') is a figure of speech that combines two nominally contradictory words or ideas. The word itself comes from a combination of the Greek terms *oxy* ('sharp') and *moros* ('dull'), so you can see where the contradictory bit comes from.

Definition

Oxymoron: *A figure of speech in which contradictory terms are conjoined so as to give point to the statement or expression. Often used loosely to mean 'contradiction in terms.'*

At school we're taught that 'oxymoron' refers to some sort of conflicting adjective – noun combination like 'old news', 'random order', 'recorded live', 'military intelligence' or 'fresh frozen'. While it's true these pairings exhibit certain oxymoronic tendencies they're not quite the real deal. Instead they shamelessly co-opt the concept of the oxymoron, bolting it onto word pairings that are basically just simple contradictions. This confusion is probably down to nothing more sinister than the fact 'oxymoron' sounds more glamorous and intellectual than 'contradiction'.

So if the likes of 'extremely average' and 'objective opinion' don't count as real oxymora, what does? Well, for the purposes of this book we'll define 'oxymoron' as the cunning use of a contradiction *to achieve a particular effect*. True oxymora usually involve two ideas that when placed in close proximity seem to gainsay each other yet are both true (unlike the simple contradictions we've just seen where one word logically opposes the other).

Just to make things more interesting, allow me to introduce a very closely related figure, the *paradox*. The main difference between the two seems to be length – paradox (again made of two Greek words – *'para'* meaning 'beyond' and *'doxa'* meaning 'opinion' or 'belief') tend to be longer and more sentence-like than oxymora, but are otherwise identical. As usual we won't worry too much about hair-splitting distinctions: oxymora, contradictions and paradox all do much the same job and as such are equally welcome here.

The oxymoron is a surprisingly useful figure, allowing writers to draw attention to some inherent ambiguity in their subject in an economical, elegant way. The Nobel Prize-winning physicist Richard Feynman, for example, once proposed a thought experiment that called for a substance he named 'dry water'. Feynman could have chosen a number of alternative phrases, including the impressive-sounding 'hydrodynamic fluids with a limiting viscosity approaching zero', but the deliberate contradiction of the phrase 'dry water' added a dash of humour (a Feynman speciality) and helped signpost the fact the substance was theoretical rather than real. The effect was to subtly imply the impossible, rendering the idea absurd, funny and above all thought provoking.

Let's have some examples of true oxymora at work:

'I must be cruel only to be kind.'
Hamlet, Act 3, Scene 4

'O modest wantons, wanton modesty!'
The Rape of Lucrece

'Damn with faint praise'
Alexander Pope

'O miserable abundance, O beggarly riches!'
John Donne

The Sounds of Silence
Simon and Garfunkel

Poor little rich girl
Shirley Temple

'I want to move with all deliberate haste'
Barack Obama

In each case the oxymoron helps invoke a fresh and vigorous image in our minds using the bare minimum of words. It stimulates our imagination by challenging us to reconcile its inherent impossibility and highlights a truth by drawing attention to its apparent absurdity. In short, oxymora get us thinking – which is, of course, exactly what they're intended to do.

So the best oxymora aren't just contradictions in terms, they're also contradictions in *ideas*. The *frisson* of the contradiction provides a novel way of describing a particular situation designed to get our synapses firing. It's here the paradoxical side of oxymora really comes into its own. In the fourth century BC Lao-Tzu, father of Taoism, wrote, 'The truest sayings are paradoxical', while in the mid 19th century Danish philosopher and theologian Søren Kierkegaard commented, 'The thinker without paradox is like a lover without feeling: a paltry mediocrity'. And more recently still Homer Simpson added, 'A boy without mischief is like a bowling ball without a liquid centre'. As far as I can tell no bowling ball has such a centre, but that doesn't stop it being a fine paradoxical phrase.

Incidentally...

It's been said that a paradox is 'a truth standing on its head to attract our attention', and I think that just about nails it. You could say exactly the same thing about oxymora in general.

More paradoxical oxymora to reflect on:

'Real knowledge is knowing the depth of one's own ignorance.'
Confucius

'Failure is the foundation of success.'
Lao-Tzu

'If it sounds like writing, I rewrite it.'
Ellmore Leonard

'Less is more.'
Mies van Der Rohe

'The more things change, the more they stay the same.'
Alphonse Karr

And:
'Oh Bart, don't worry, people die all the time. In fact, you could wake up dead tomorrow.'
Homer Simpson

Incidentally...

Mies van Der Rohe borrowed 'Less is more' from Robert Browning's 1855 poem Men and Women. *Browning in turn had lifted it from 18th century German poet Christoph Martin Wieland, who credited another German writer, Gotthold Lessing, with its creation. Such is the way with soundbites.*

Each is an example of what's sometimes called a 'self-cancelling phrase'. By opposing what we instinctively know to be true, these oxymora jolt us into paying attention. Mies van Der Rohe could have said, 'Keep stuff simple' instead of 'Less is more' – it makes much the same point, but it lacks the style and provocation of his phrase.

So paradox gives language power. Film titles like *Back to the Future*, *True Lies* and *Eyes Wide Shut* cause us to look twice because they offend our semantic sensibilities – 'What do they mean, *True Lies*?? That's…that's…impossible! I'd better watch it to find out what they're on about.' Kemal Ataturk, the father of modern, secular Turkey, wanted to encourage women to dispense with the traditional Islamic veil. Instead of tackling the problem head-on and provoking a fight, he issued an edict that read, 'All prostitutes must wear veils', (something they were forbidden to do at the time). Paradoxically the problem was solved not by forbidding veils, but by insisting on them.

Legendary 1980s London estate agent Roy Brooke sold more property than you could shake a stick at by telling the unadorned truth. He minced no words and spared no feelings. For example:

Darkest Pimlico. *Seedy FAMILY HOUSE two rooms in the basement, ground, 1st & 2nd floors and attic rm. on 3rd. Decor! Peeling, faded and fly blown. Garden – good G.R. £60 p.a. £6,950. If you are too late to secure this gem we have a spare along the road rather more derelict. A lightly built member of our staff negotiated the basement stair but our Mr Halstead went crashing through.*

I mention all this because it shows how trying the exact opposite of what's expected can yield elegant answers to tough problems. It's another example of the 'contradiction of ideas' theme we met a moment ago.

One way to use this approach in business communications is to give credit where credit's due with your competition. If they're cheaper, faster or better than you, *say so*. It establishes trust with your audience, differentiates you from the competition (who presumably all knock each other) and shows supreme confidence in your abilities. Just don't forget to sell yourself somewhere along the line. Similarly, if there's some weakness in your offer, state it clearly before the customer finds out from another source – that way you can control the debate, build your credibility, establish a reputation for scrupulous honesty *and* get a counter argument in early.

Another business writing example that may amuse and certainly shows that honesty can be a great attention grabber was a recent 'call for entries' form for the Singapore Creative Circle annual advertising awards. As is usual with such documents, it began by asking for the:

- *Nominated advert:*
- *Agency involved:*
- *Art director and writer responsible for the ad:*

Without missing a beat it then went on to ask:

- *Guy in the room at the time:*
- *Creative Director who didn't understand the idea but is now taking all the credit:*
- *Finance person who said there was no money in awards:*
- *Freelancer who said it was all his idea:*
- *Other creatives who managed to get their name associated with it:*
- *Account handler whose brief had nothing to do with the final ad:*

By mocking the proliferation of names that tend to attach themselves to successful adverts, this simple little form stood out and achieved its intended effect with admirable economy. As Homer Simpson would say, 'It's funny 'cos it's true.'

So, rather than think of oxymora and paradoxes as contradictions that highlight some shortcoming or oddity for comic or satirical effect, these freaky phrases actually highlight the highest (or should that be deepest?) truths. It's at this point that oxymora segue neatly into our next figure: irony. Both involve saying the opposite of what we really mean in the hope that our audience will glimpse something more. Let us proceed.

IRONY
'THEY COULDN'T HIT AN ELEPHANT AT THIS DIST—'*

Definition
Irony: *A figure of speech in which emphasis is placed on the opposition between the literal and intended meaning of a statement.*

In the world of irony things are not as they seem. Cicero described it as, 'saying one thing and meaning another', which certainly captures one sense of the word, but as J.A. Cuddon says in *A Dictionary of Literary Terms and Literary Theory,* irony 'eludes definition' and 'this elusiveness is one of the main reasons why it is a source of so much fascinated inquiry and speculation.' Let the inquiry and speculation begin.

---

* The immortal words of American Civil War General John Sedgwick, immediatley prior to being shot and killed by a Confederate sniper.

Elizabethan poet George Puttenham translated the Latin word 'ironia' as 'drie mock', a beautiful, evocative phrase that makes a similar point to Cicero but with infinitely more eloquence. Building on this translation, Robertson Davis wrote, 'The ironist is not bitter, he does not seek to undercut everything that seems worthy or serious, he scorns the cheap scoring-off of the wisecracker. He stands, so to speak, somewhat at one side, observes and speaks with a moderation which is occasionally embellished with a flash of controlled exaggeration.'

When we talk about irony in this way there's a quietly humorous inconsistency or incongruity at work, in which an apparently straightforward statement is undercut by its context to yield a very different meaning. For example, in the famous 'lend me your ears' speech from Shakespeare's *Julius Caesar*, Mark Anthony seems to be praising the conspirators who killed Caesar when in fact he is quietly condemning them with lines like:

'Yet Brutus says he was ambitious;
And Brutus is an honourable man.'
Act 3, Scene 2

We're left in no doubt as to who's ambitious and who's honourable. The literal truth of what's written clashes with the perceived truth of what's meant to revealing effect, which is irony in a nutshell.

Incidentally...
We use the phrase 'tongue in cheek' to describe anything with ironic overtones. The phrase is obscure in origin, but may have originated in the 18ᵗʰ century to describe the facial contortions of Spanish nobility as they tried to suppress their mirth at the foolery of their minstrels. It didn't appear in the OED until 1933, which is odd because Sir Walter Scott used it in the modern sense in his novel The Fair Maid of Perth *in 1828.*

A common misconception is that 'ironic' is a direct synonym for 'coincidental'. The lyrics of Alanis Morissette's UK top 11 (and US top five) hit *Ironic* describe a number of apparently ironic situations, each verse ending with the refrain, 'Isn't It Ironic?' To which the answer must be a polite but firm 'no', as the lyrics are in fact a succinct explanation of what irony *isn't*. How ironic. For example she writes, 'An old man turned 98, he won the lottery and died the next day', which is just plain sad. Another line – 'It's like rain on your wedding day' – seems to mistake irony for the weather, while, 'A traffic jam when you're already late' suggests failing transport policies rather than figures of speech.

Please don't think me a pedant, but such is Alanis' catalogue of irony errors that it's impossible to avoid the suspicion she was doing it deliberately. Here's what the woman herself had to say on the subject:

'For me the great debate on whether what I was saying in Ironic was ironic wasn't a traumatic debate. I'd always embraced the fact that every once in a while I'd be the malapropism queen. And when we were writing it, we definitely were not doggedly making sure that everything was technically ironic.'

Translation: I couldn't be arsed. That's fair enough, but she also got 'malapropism' wrong, which is just taking the piss. As the comedian Ed Byrne has deliciously pointed out: 'The only ironic thing about that song is it's called *Ironic* and it's written by a woman who doesn't know what irony is. That's quite ironic.'

Irony comes in various subtly different forms according to its function, all of which richly repay closer scrutiny. The first form we'll examine, *verbal irony,* is the classic spoken or written form that involves a discrepancy of expression and intention as described above.

Verbal irony appears in many forms of literature, from the tragedies of Sophocles to the novels of Jane Austen, but it's an especially important ingredient in satire. One of the most famous examples comes from 18th century English writer Jonathan Swift. In a pamphlet called *A Modest Proposal* he suggested that the poor of Ireland could rid themselves of their poverty by selling their unwanted children to the rich as food. He goes into great detail about the many and various advantages to his scheme and even suggests cooking techniques: 'A young healthy child well nursed is at a year old a most delicious, nourishing, and wholesome food, whether stewed, roasted, baked, or boiled; and I make no doubt that it will equally serve in a fricassee or a ragout'. It's one of the all-time classic texts in the history of irony, largely because Swift's tone is completely deadpan – there's no authorial wink to suggest, 'Hey, I'm joking' Instead it's up to the reader to work out what's going on.

Next, *dramatic irony,* the name given to any situation in film, TV, theatre or literature where the audience understands the significance of some particular words or actions but the characters don't. Dramatic irony puts the audience ahead of the plot in some way, usually with privileged information unavailable to those caught up in the narrative. Writers use it to make the audience cringe, cheer or laugh. It's that, 'No! Don't go in there!' reaction we have when we see Scooby and Shaggy head into the abandoned fairground that's home to an improbable swamp monster who hates hippies and talking dogs. On a more refined level, it also described the final scene in Shakespeare's *Romeo and Juliet* where Romeo finds Juliet in a drugged sleep, assumes that she's dead and kills himself, only for Juliet to wake up, discover what's happened, and then her to kill herself too.

Incidentally...

Jane Austen's Pride and Prejudice *begins with the famous proposition 'It is a truth universally acknowledged, that a single man in possession of a good fortune, must be in want of a wife.' It soon becomes clear that Austen means the opposite: women (or more often their mothers) are always on the lookout for a rich single man to make a husband.*

Next, the marvellously named *cosmic* (or *situational*) *irony,* the phenomenon Alanis Morrisette was getting at in the aforementioned song. It's a relatively recent deployment of the 'I' word and describes any discrepancy between expected and actual results. It's been defined as 'perverse appropriateness', where the result of an action is contrary to the desired or expected effect, highlighting the disparity between human desires and the harsh realities of our heartless world.

Let's have some examples of situational or cosmic irony in action. The first concerns fatal US astronaut Gus Grissom. On splashing down in the Pacific after his first space fight in 1961 the hatch on his capsule fell off and Gus nearly drowned. The hatch was completely redesigned to prevent such a situation ever happening again. A few years later Gus was preparing for a test flight of Apollo One when a fire broke out in the command module just prior to launch and Grissom and two other astronauts suffocated. The changes in hatch design – intended to save lives – fatally delayed their rescue.

Similarly, Jim Fixx, the man who did much to popularise jogging as a form of healthy exercise with his 1977 best seller *The Complete Book of Running*, died at the age of 52 of a heart attack – a condition typically associated with sedentary, unhealthy lifestyles – while out, yep, you guessed it, jogging.

Then there's *The Wizard of Oz*. Dorothy completes all the Wizard's challenges in order to go home, only to discover she could have done so whenever she wanted. Likewise, the Scarecrow longs for intelligence, only to discover he's already a genius, the Tin Man longs to be capable of love, only to discover he already has a heart, while the terminally timorous Lion turns out to be boldness personified.

Finally, let me mention John Hinckley, who in 1981 made a botched attempt to assassinate President Ronald Reagan. All Hinckley's shots missed the president, however one slug ricocheted off the bullet-proof presidential limousine and hit Reagan in the chest. So a vehicle made to *protect* the President from gunfire was partially responsible for his being shot.

The final type of irony we'll examine is perhaps the most useful for business writers – *Socratic irony*. This involves adopting a mask of innocence and/or ignorance in order to expose weaknesses in your opponent's argument. In practice this might mean something as simple as repeating, 'I honestly don't understand, explain it to me again', when faced with an unpalatable or unworkable suggestion. The more its author is forced to examine and restate their idea, the more its cracks will start to show, at which point you can quietly point out the error of their ways and carry the day.

Ironically...

Staying with the somewhat niche theme of irony and presidential assassinations, let's rewind to Dallas, 22nd November 1963. While riding in the same car as JFK, Mrs Connolly, wife of the Texas Governor, remarked, 'Mr President, you can't say that Dallas doesn't love you'. Kennedy replied, 'That's certainly true'. Moments later he was dead.

Socrates himself regularly pretended to admire the wisdom of his opponent. His 'innocent' enquiries ruthlessly revealed the vanity or foolishness of his opponent's proposition, usually through gentle questioning of their basic assumptions. The process greatly entertained onlookers who knew that Socrates was wiser than he allowed himself to appear and who spotted the direction the naive questioning was taking. It's just as effective today. Socratic irony, an elegant, ingenious and unfailingly polite method of interrogation, is perfect for discussing and debating dogmas without descending into fisticuffs.

TV journalist Louis Theroux is an expert in the use of Socratic irony. By approaching his subjects with an air of cosy naivety and admiring curiosity he encourages them to drop their guard in a way no adversarial approach could hope to achieve.

Sacha Baron Cohen's character Ali G also uses Socratic irony for satirical effect. While interviewing a professor from the National Poison Information Centre about recreational drug use he asked, 'Does Class A drugs absolutely guarantee that they is better quality?', which yielded a detailed response that made drugs sound like any other consumer product, which was presumably the point. By getting his interviewee to agree to some breathtaking inaccuracy or follow an absurd line of thinking he helps them highlight issues they'd probably prefer to gloss over. A fine example occurred when probing the Bishop of Horsham about God's physical appearance; the bishop, understandably exasperated, replied rather creatively, 'Well, he's sort of Jesus-shaped'.

Yet despite its many good points all is not well in the world of irony. Always an intangible idea, in the last few decades the idea of what constitutes irony has expanded and sprawled so that it's become all things to all men, meaning whatever each of us says it means. In an article in *Time* magazine called *The Age of Irony Comes to an End* published immediately after the events of 9/11, writer Roger Rosenblatt had this to say:

> *'One good thing could come from this horror: it could spell the end of the age of irony. For some 30 years – roughly as long as the Twin Towers were upright – the good folks in charge of America's intellectual life have insisted that nothing was to be believed in or taken seriously.*

*Nothing was real. With a giggle and a smirk, our chattering classes –
our columnists and pop culture makers – declared that detachment
and personal whimsy were the necessary tools for an oh-so-cool life.
Who but a slobbering bumpkin would think, "I feel your pain"? The
ironists, seeing through everything, made it difficult for anyone to see
anything. The consequence of thinking that nothing is real – apart from
prancing around in an air of vain stupidity – is that one will not know the
difference between a joke and a menace. No more. The planes that
plowed into the World Trade Center and the Pentagon were real. The
flames, smoke, sirens – real. The chalky landscape, the silence of the
streets – all real. I feel your pain – really.'*

Likewise, Jon Winokur, author of *The Big Book of Irony*, pitched in with:
*'Postmodern irony is allusive, multilayered, pre-emptive, cynical, and
above all, nihilistic. It assumes that everything is subjective and nothing
means what it says. It's a sneering, world-weary, bad irony, a mentality
that condemns before it can be condemned, preferring cleverness to
sincerity and quotation to originality. Postmodern irony rejects tradition,
but offers nothing in its place.'*

Too much irony undoubtedly leaves us a little queasy, but isn't their
blanket rejection a baby/bathwater situation? Irony isn't all bad, as we've
seen in the examples above. Zoe Williams, writing in *The Guardian* in
2003, made the case for the defence:
*'There are a number of misconceptions about irony that are peculiar to
recent times. The first is that September 11 spelled the end of irony.
The second is that the end of irony would be the one good thing to
come out of September 11. The third is that irony characterizes our age
to a greater degree than it has done any other. The fourth is that Americans can't do irony, and we [the British] can. The fifth is that the
Germans can't do irony, either (and we still can). The sixth is that irony
and cynicism are interchangeable. The seventh is that it's a mistake to
attempt irony in emails and text messages, even while irony characterises our age, and so do emails. And the eighth is that "post-ironic" is an*

acceptable term – it is very modish to use this, as if to suggest one of three things: i) that irony has ended; ii) that postmodernism and irony are interchangeable, and can be conflated into one handy word; or iii) that we are more ironic than we used to be, and therefore need to add a prefix suggesting even greater ironic distance than irony on its own can supply. None of these things is true.'

It's good to see the tired old chestnut about Americans not appreciating irony being put out to grass (if you'll excuse my mixed grass/chestnut metaphor). Simon Pegg – comedian and star of *Shaun Of The Dead* and *Hot Fuzz* – said of irony, 'Americans just don't feel entirely comfortable using it on each other, in case it causes damage. A bit like how we feel about guns'.

Before we wrap up, a couple of points about the value of irony in business communications. If you need to overcome sales resistance (and I use 'sales' in the broad sense of getting someone to buy into *something*, whether it's an idea, a political ideology or a new brand of nasal hair trimmer), one way to do it is to openly concede that you're trying to manipulate your audience. Just say it clearly at the start of your spiel. By displaying a modicum of honesty you stand a better chance of gaining their trust, at least temporarily. What you're doing is openly acknowledging that *all* rhetorical manoeuvring is ironic, in that it says one thing while meaning another. By these magical means irony can help you to bond with your audience and win their consent, although be warned that once you start down this road the irony starts to run away with itself: 'I want you to agree with me so I'm being honest about trying to manipulate you, but that honesty is itself a technique to get you to agree with me…'.

Likewise, irony can produce hard-hitting headlines that don't seem to say much when read out of context but pack a serious wallop when combined with imagery. An award-winning advert for the American Cancer Society showed a black-and-white photograph of a graveyard over the headline, 'Welcome to Marlboro Country'. Similarly, the Partnership for a Drug-Free America ran an ad featuring a straightforward headline that read, 'One of the surest ways to get your message across is to put celebrities in your ad'. The picture was a montage featuring Jimi Hendrix, Janis

Joplin, River Phoenix and John Belushi – all celebrities and all very dead thanks to their involvement with drugs.

A similar and even more economical line was used in a great advert for a Scottish undertakers:

'Thank you for smoking.'

Using nothing more than white text on a black background this print ad raised awareness about the dangers of cigarettes while simultaneously and ironically thanking smokers for their future custom. Similar and equally ironic anti-smoking ad lines include:

'For more information on lung cancer, keep smoking.'

And the no-nonsense:

'Cancer cures smoking'

Finally, I can't resist mentioning this brilliantly written radio advert for Stonewall, the group that campaigns for equality, fairness and safety on behalf of the non-hetero population. It employed irony to highly amusing effect and began:

Gay son: Mum, Dad, I'm gay.
Dad: YES!!!
Mum: O-my-God, O-my-God, O-my-God, we've got a gay son!! Wait until I tell my sister! She's going to be so jealous.
Dad: I don't want to get my hopes up. You sure you're gay?

Before ending:

Dad: Hey, Reverend Wallis! Didn't see you standing in the porch there. I have a gay son!
Reverend: I heard and I just want you to know that God loves him and the Church accepts him with open arms.
Dad: Sweet!

The final voice-over nails the irony with admirable restraint:

Until the world is a little more like this, we're here.

SARCASM
A SECTION ON SARCASM, THAT'S *JUST* WHAT WE NEED...

Closely related to irony is *sarcasm*, the name we give to mocking remarks made to poke fun at others. The difference between these two figures centres on intent – irony simply *is*, whereas sarcasm – even the humorous

Definition

Sarcasm: *A form of wit marked by the use of satirical language to make its victim the butt of contempt or ridicule.*

variety – normally has a malign objective. What's more, sarcasm aims to be funny whereas irony ain't necessarily so. Irony also tends to be rather more sophisticated (the more sophisticated the irony, the more it's implied rather than stated) whereas sarcasm is inevitably direct.

Some commentators consider sarcasm to be a cruder, lower form of irony, or simply a subspecies of verbal irony. But sarcasm always hinges on the speaker; a *person* is sarcastic (a *sarcast*), but a *situation* is ironic.

Unlike irony, sarcasm is never deceptive, although we don't always grasp the sarcast's true intention right away.

Sarcasm tends to involve a particular kind of personal criticism. It's frequently bitter, often cutting and generally intended to wound. No surprise therefore, that the word itself comes from the Greek for 'tear the flesh' or 'bite the lips in rage', in reference to its taunting nature.

Incidentally...

Sarcasm is an example of what some researchers call 'unplain speaking' in which what is said differs fundamentally from what is meant. This category of language also includes forced politeness, ritual language, affectation and speaking in aphorisms. Think of it as 'I say this, but I mean that'.

The word 'sarcasm' first appeared in a 1579 poem called *The Shepheardes Calender* by Edmund Spenser:

> *'An Ironicall [Sarcasmus], spoken in derision of these rude wits, whych make more account of a ryming rybaud, then of skill grounded vpon learning and iudgment.'*

A few years later Henry Peacham included this cautionary remark in *The Garden of Eloquence:*

> *'Let it be first provided that this figure (sarcasmus) be not used without some great cause which may well deserve it, as arrogancie, insolent*

pride, wilfull folly, shamefull lecherie, ridiculous avarice, or such like, for it is both folly and rudenesse to use derision without cause: but to mocke silly people, innocents, or men in misery, or the poore in distresse, argueth both the pride of the mind, and the crueltie of the heart.'

Old though these quotes are, the use of sarcasm goes back much further:
Lo, you see the man is mad; why then have you brought him to me? Do I lack madmen, that you have brought this fellow to play the madman in my presence?
I Sam 21:10-15

And when the prophets of Baal fail to call down fire from heaven in a contest with Elijah:
He mocked them, and said, Cry aloud: for he is a god; either he is talking, or he is pursuing, or he is in a journey, or peradventure he sleepeth, and must be awaked.
1 Kings 18:27

While Shakespeare – as usual – had something to say on the subject:
Thrift, thrift, Horatio! The funeral bak'd meats did coldly furnish forth the marriage tables.
Hamlet Act 1, Scene 2

Where Hamlet is congratulating his uncle and mother for their thriftiness while sarcastically pointing out that his father's funeral was barely over before their wedding began.

Sarcasm is so ubiquitous these days it almost goes unnoticed. When someone makes a non-joke at our expense what do we say? 'Very funny' (without cracking a smile). When the cat suffers an upset tummy on the shagpile how do we reply? 'That's all I need.' Some phrases are only *ever* used sarcastically: 'My heart bleeds', 'Wise guy', 'My hero', 'Big deal', 'Our beloved leader' (in Britain, anyway), while other phrases have been used sarcastically for so long they now mean the opposite of their original meaning. For example, 'Too bad,' was once an expression of sympathy before the sarcastic crowd got their hands on it.

Sarcasm divides the court of public opinion. The case for the prosecution is that it can be downright rude – the verbal equivalent of pointing and laughing. Simply saying the opposite of what you mean doesn't count as razor-sharp repartee worthy of the Algonquin Round Table.

The case for the defence hinges on how sarcasm can be a brilliant, artful, learned thing. Almost all humour is at someone's expense (even the self-depreciating kind), so guilt isn't really the issue. The trick is to use sarcasm intelligently and sparingly. After all, there is no reason why sarcasm has to be dumb – just as there are cool and corny metaphors, there are cool and corny examples of sarcasm – so learn to use sarcasm as an effective comment on the slings and arrows of outrageous fortune. Despite all that stuff about it being the lowest form of wit (which, as we saw in Chapter 5, is a misquote of Dr Johnson's opinion of puns) sarcasm can be outrageously funny, as these examples from a series of masters show. First, Groucho Marx:

Incidentally...

If you suffer from a sense of humour failure when confronted by an over-sarcastic colleague then act dumb. Fail to understand their point by taking everything they say at face value (more than a hint of Socratic irony here). If their opening gambit is something like, 'Well that's all I need' you could parry with, 'Really? Oh good. I thought you'd be angry I just reformatted the server.' Smile, play it straight and don't overdo it.

'No, Groucho is not my real name. I am breaking it in for a friend.'

'I never forget a face, but in your case I'll be glad to make an exception.'

'I find television very educating. Every time somebody turns on the set, I go into the other room and read a book.'

'I have had a perfectly wonderful evening, but this wasn't it.'

'I didn't like the play, but then I saw it under adverse conditions – the curtain was up.'

Now let's have some Mark Twain:
'I didn't attend the funeral, but I sent a nice letter saying I approved of it.'

'Honesty is the best policy – when there is money in it.'

'Reader, suppose you were an idiot. And suppose you were a member of Congress. But I repeat myself.'

'I would like to live in Manchester, England. The transition between Manchester and death would be unnoticeable.'

Then there's Jane Austen's, 'You have delighted us long enough', and Churchill's cutting analysis of Clement Attlee, 'A modest man, who has much to be modest about.' No scrutiny of sarcasm would be complete without some words from Basil Fawlty. When a hard-to-please guest complains about the view from her window he responds:
'What did you expect to see out of a Torquay hotel bedroom window? Sydney Opera House perhaps? The Hanging Gardens of Babylon? Herds of wildebeest sweeping majestically across the plains?'

And finally this from filmmaker and professional irritant Michael Moore. Less sophisticated but still funny:
'I would like to apologize for referring to George W. Bush as a deserter. What I meant to say is that George W. Bush is a deserter, an election thief, a drunk driver, a WMD liar, and a functional illiterate. And he poops his pants.'

For sarcasm to work your audience has to be in on the joke – if you need to tell them it's sarcasm it instantly isn't. And even if they're willing, not everyone will get it. Sarcasm is one of the last and most advanced verbal concepts children learn. In fact they often don't really grasp it until the age of twelve and sometimes much later. With really young kids it's a non-starter:

'My, Eva, I just love what you've done to your bib! Andrew, come and look! Porridge would look great added to that vomit, why don't you give it a go...'

It's not just the very young who are confused, as this from Sir Alex Ferguson makes clear:

'Never use sarcasm on players. It doesn't work.'

BABIES AND SARCASM DON'T MIX.

So troublesome is this issue of not getting it when sarcasm is written rather than spoken (without the benefit of intonation to guide interpretation) that in some Ethiopic languages sarcasm is indicated with a special sarcasm mark. This looks like a backwards question mark at the end of a sentence and is surprisingly like French poet Alcanter de Brahm's proposed irony mark (؟). In some situations (such as subtitles and TV's Teletext) modern writers have adopted the convention of using an exclamation mark in brackets to indicate sarcasm. Yet still the problem persists, particularly so in the online world where ways of indicating sarcasm on the web include bolding the stressed word, putting it in 'quotation' marks or even using <sarcasm> faux tags </sarcasm>. How clever (!).

Be all that as it may, what has sarcasm got to offer business communicators? One particularly fine answer to that question comes in the form of a press ad run by Lothian and Borders Fire Brigade designed to promote the installation of home smoke alarms. It was a deliberately low budget, text-only affair that mimicked a certain sort of market research advert. The banner headline read, 'Are you dead? Did you die in a house fire? If so we'd love to hear from you!' Under which were a series of bullet points:

- What's it like being burnt to death?
- Did it hurt?
- Did you smell like chicken?
- The afterlife – where's good?
- Do you know Elvis?
- Still got your "whatever happens, happens" attitude?

Before ending on:

- Do you regret not spending £5 on a smoke alarm?

By treating this most serious of subjects in a light-hearted way the writers poked fun at people who do exactly the same thing at home, underscoring their stupidity and making a truly memorable message at the same time. The lesson is that sarcasm can be used positively to make a point

– all it takes is a little imagination and the confidence to be rude where it counts.

Another, far milder example comes courtesy of Virgin Atlantic. Intended to highlight their excellent in-flight entertainment, this ad took the form of a spoof movie poster featuring a large picture of a sweet old lady and the movie title *Stories about my grandchildren* with the strapline, 'Brought to you by the elderly lady in seat 4C'. Two other snippets of text read, 'You look like a nice young man...' and 'You won't be able to get away', all of which was contrasted with the selling line of 'Not every airline has 55 channels of in-flight entertainment'. The message was that if you want to avoid being button-holed on long haul flights by fellow travellers and their stories of dubious interest you'd better fly with Virgin. Gently poking fun at the tendency of grandparents to ramble on about grandchildren allowed this ad to make its point in an amiable, engaging way.

My final example of sarcasm in business writing comes in the form of press ads for Edinburgh furniture store Martin & Frost. A series of these appeared on the TV listings pages of several regional papers. Each used the same headline – *Avoid Today* – and then went on to highlight some horror that was part of that day's TV fodder, before ending with a recommendation that the viewer would be far better off forgoing said show and popping down to Martin & Frost instead.

For example, the ad warning viewers to avoid a rerun of Miami Vice read, 'Forget the murders, try solving the crimes against furniture', complaining that Miami Vice inflicted 'waterbeds, white PVC sofas and gold dining tables' upon its long-suffering audience, before closing with the advice that viewers would be better off 'heading down to Martin & Frost and investing in some timeless furniture. Case closed.' By making their sarcasm entertaining and extremely topical the writers got the reader on their side in record time – half the battle when it comes to making a sale.

IN A NUTSHELL
TOP TIPS FOR BUSINESS WRITERS

- Use oxymora and paradox to draw attention to your subject in an economical, elegant way. Don't limit yourself to word pairings, instead try combining ideas that seem to contradict each other yet are both true. The result is often a bright, energetic image achieved using the minimum of words.

- Disarming honesty – to the point of deliberately highlighting some shortcomings in your subject – is the opposite of what cynical audiences expect. As ace American ad man Bill Bernbach once said, 'I've got a great gimmick. Let's tell the truth'.

- Irony makes for high impact headlines, especially in situations where it's permissible to mock the reader's folly. Socratic irony is a tried and true method of highlighting the shortcomings of an opponent's argument.

- Sarcasm turns up the volume on irony and can be useful when you need to talk about something serious, unpleasant or just plain boring in a way that gets past people's mental defences. Don't go overboard – a little dab of sarcasm goes a long way.

CHAPTER EIGHT

BRINGING IT ALL TOGETHER

HOW RHETORIC CAN ROCK THE BUSINESS WRITER'S WORLD

No discussion of figures of speech would be complete without some mention of rhetoric, the Classical 'art of persuasion' designed to influence the judgment and feelings of others. Developed by Greek and Roman thinkers in the half millennium before Christ, rhetoric (from the Greek for 'that which is spoken') was a complete, end-to-end technique for effective communication. Great Classical rhetoricians like Aristotle and Cicero documented their techniques in what are basically 'how to' guides for giving a great speech (although their ideas apply equally well to writing). Cicero in particular systemised the art of rhetoric into five parts or *canons*: invention (thinking what to say), arrangement (crafting your argument for maximum effect), style (how you express your ideas), delivery (speaking well on the day) and memory (actually remembering your lines). Figures of speech belong to the canon of style whose function it was to present the raw facts of an argument in the most appealing and effective way possible. Put it like that and rhetoric's relevance to business writing becomes clear.

Incidentally...

Cicero met a distinctly grisly end. Mark Anthony had him assassinated and his head and hands nailed up in the Forum. Fulvia, Anthony's wife, then repeatedly (and very publicly) stuck her gold hairpin through the dead man's tongue specifically to take vengeance on his power of speech. That gives you some idea of what these people thought of rhetoric and its ability to shape events.

Rhetoric's aim was pleasingly simple: to present a case in such a compelling way that the audience couldn't help but come around to your way of thinking. As the great ad man (and recipient of an expensive Classical education), David Ogilvy put it, 'When Aeschines spoke, they said, "How well he speaks", but when Demosthenes spoke, they said, "Let us march against Philip!"' As business writers we want to get our readers marching not admiring, and rhetoric is the way to do it.

The ancients were queuing up to give rhetoric the thumbs up. Plato believed that rhetoric was the 'art of enchanting the soul', while Aristotle defined rhetoric as 'the faculty of discovering in any particular case all of the available means of persuasion'. Quintillion pronounced, 'rhetoric is the art of speaking well', while Cicero described it as 'to prove, to please and to persuade'. The Roman era was rhetoric's heyday – sadly it was all downhill from there. Despite a revival of interest in the Renaissance (hence Henry Peacham's *The Garden of Eloquence*, the inspiration behind this book), by the mid 18th century John Locke felt able to describe rhetoric as, 'that powerful instrument of error and deceit.' Today it's often used as a pejorative term associated with windy argument at best and downright manipulation at worst.

How did this fall from grace occur? Alas, it all started with Aristotle, one of rhetoric's most effective exponents. He argued that rhetoric's job was to prove a point *or give the impression of proving it*. That last bit was (and remains) crucial; it's the basis of the charge that rhetoric isn't concerned with right or wrong, just winning arguments by all means necessary. A whiff of suspicion concerning rhetoric's potential to perform a 'slight of words' has clung to it ever since, reaching its apogee in the 20th century, as these quotes show:

'The broad masses of a population are more amenable to the appeal of rhetoric than to any other force.'
Adolf Hitler

'Rhetoric is a poor substitute for action. If we are really to be a great nation, we must not merely talk; we must act big.'
Theodore Roosevelt

'The truth is, President Bush provides the right rhetoric, but then pursues all the wrong policies.'
Senator John Kerry

You won't be surprised to hear I consider this grossly unfair: rhetoric doesn't kill people; people do. It's just as easy to use rhetoric's techniques for good as for evil. Imagine how much better the world would be if right could triumph over might through eloquent argument alone – exactly the situation rhetoric tries to bring about. The sad fact that it sometimes fails in this noble aim is more to do with human nature and vested interests than shortcomings in the idea itself.

THREE WAYS TO PERSUADE
WHAT *ETHOS*, *PATHOS* AND *LOGOS* CAN DO FOR YOU

Let us thumb our noses at these ill-informed objections and look more closely at the mechanics of rhetoric.

Among the many important rhetorical ideas he formulated, Aristotle gave us the concept of three 'modes of persuasion': *ethos*, *pathos* and *logos*. These three little words contain a multitude of ideas that are relevant to all writers whose job it is to sell with words. Let's cast a brisk eye over all three.

The closest English equivalent to the Greek word *ethos* is probably 'image' – the way the writer presents himself to the reader in the text. To demonstrate how ethos is a key part of persuasion, I present an excerpt from a speech delivered in 1952 by a young senator from California named Richard Nixon who was suspected of benefiting from an illegal slush fund. Nixon went on TV to defend himself in what became known as the 'Checkers Speech' because it ends with a heart warming (or stomach turning, depending on your point of view) anecdote about a cute black and white spaniel called Checkers. Here's how he began his televisual defence:

'I was born in 1913. Our family was one of modest circumstances and most of my early life was spent in a store out in East Whittier. It was a grocery store – one of those family enterprises. The only reason we were able to make it go was because my mother and dad had five boys and we all worked in the store. I worked my way through college and to a great extent through law school. And then, in 1940, probably the best thing that ever happened to me happened, I married Pat – who is sitting over here. We had a rather difficult time after we were married, like so many of the young couples who may be listening to us. I practiced law;

she continued to teach school. Then in 1942 I went into the service. Let me say that my service record was not a particularly unusual one. I went to the South Pacific. I guess I'm entitled to a couple of battle stars. I got a couple of letters of commendation but I was just there when the bombs were falling and then I returned. I returned to the United States and in 1946 I ran for the Congress.'

In this first paragraph Nixon very deliberately sets out to identify himself with his imagined audience. He establishes himself as a family man, as a hard worker, a committed husband, as someone who ('like so many of the young couples who may be listening to us') had a tough time financially, and as a modest but brave patriot who fought in the Second World War (that stuff about the battle stars). It's basically a list of mainstream American values designed to establish his ethos by convincing the American people (and his boss, Eisenhower) that he was honest and trustworthy. It worked like a charm; Nixon wriggled off the hook and was free to carry on conniving until his eventual downfall in the Watergate scandal 22 years later.

As with dirty politicians, so with business writers – both need to be aware of ethos and its power to persuade (although hopefully that's the only thing they share). Indeed, the writer who neglects how he or she comes over in print is courting disaster. For a business writer concerned with establishing an organisation's point of difference, bona fides and personality the best advice I can give is, *don't claim: demonstrate.* Offer your reader tangible proof of your point but without signposting it as such – the subtler your demonstration of ethos the more effective it will be (although to be fair Nixon's efforts were as subtle as a knee in the groin). What form should your proof take? Well, facts are the most potent persuaders in your arsenal – if you've got numbers or other evidence available to substantiate your argument then use them. Next come percentages and other relative comparisons, followed in a rather poor third by endorsements, quotes or other claims. In summary, a few well-chosen facts, presented with a lightness of touch, will do wonders for your ethos.

Now *pathos*. In the context of rhetoric, pathos (from the Greek for 'emotion') is about making an appeal to your audience's feeling, or, as Aristotle put it, 'creating a certain disposition'. It's hard to overstate the power of pathos in effective business communication. When a business writer sets out to rouse a sense of desire, curiosity, excitement or any other emotion in their readers, they're making a deliberate appeal to their audience's emotions; in other words they're invoking pathos. Far from being an obscure part of an ancient debating technique, pathos is part and parcel of the 21ˢᵗ century marketing landscape.

Incidentally...

In the world of art, pathos means invoking a sense of sympathy or pity, but that's a modern re-definition of its original meaning.

The key to getting this right is to know your audience and write with them in mind. Inexperienced writers often assume that everyone either already thinks the way they do or that they will once they've finished the piece. Sadly this is rarely the case. My advice is, *remember your reader*. If the language you use and the ideas you choose to present are wrong for your reader, then all the eloquence in the world won't help. In fact, an understanding of your audience should be the first thing you think of when trying to determine the right way to appeal to their emotions. Visualise the person you want to write to and speak to them as if they're sitting across the table. Picture them in as much detail as you can muster. What's on their mind? What makes them excited? Fearful? Bored? Motivated? How can you get around the inevitable 'so what' question? How can you answer the 'what's in it for me' enquiry? Only by doing this can you be sure you won't solve the wrong problem when you come to write.

Interestingly...

Kenneth Burke, expert on all things rhetorical and author of A Grammar of Motives *puts it this way, 'You persuade a man only in so far as you can talk his language by speech, gesture, tonality, order, image, attitude, idea, identifying your ways with his.' Know your audience should be the first lesson every business writer learns because that's how they can appeal to their reader's pathos.*

Finally *logos*. Aristotle was convinced that the core of an argument was its logic. This, however, is where I must disagree with the great man. I think we can be fairly sure Aristotle never had to pen a series of dog food ads intended to attract the attention of sceptical pet owners in a saturated market. Nor did he involve himself with internal communications, investor relations, brand building or product positioning – all typical tasks for today's business writers. If he had, I like to think he'd feel more as I do and recognise that emotion plays a massive role in our day-to-day decision making.

Allow me to explain. If you're a business writer, you're trying to win an argument. By 'argument' I clearly don't mean a heated post-pub debate on the merits of playing a 4:2:4 formation against the Germans; I mean a process in which you engage with a number of people in order to make a point and convince them of the worth of a particular product, service or point of view. It's selling, but *soft* selling as it's about winning with ideas.

It's been said that business writing is basically 'salesmanship in print'.

Interestingly...

Raymond K. Price, one of the architects of President Nixon's election success in 1968, is reported to have declared in the early stages of the campaign that rational arguments would 'only be effective if we get people to make the emotional leap...' That's exactly what business writers need to do, and figures of speech are how they can do it.

That's certainly part of the story but not the whole thing. Take this approach too far and pretty soon business copy becomes cold and unconvincing. People rarely buy for wholly rational reasons, and in many cases writing that contains an emotional element will outperform its rational relation. *Good business writing almost always appeals to its readers for reasons other than pure reason* – in other words a hardcore 'reasons to believe' approach based on Aristotle's logos must be tempered with whatever it takes to capture the reader's imagination, and that usually means introducing something softer and more subjective. In short, you neglect the emotional at your peril.

PUTTING RHETORIC INTO PRACTICE
SEVEN TECHNIQUES TO GET YOU STARTED

By now you might be thinking, 'Enough already, I get it – figures of speech help bring business language to life, but how do I put all this into practice? Where do I begin?' The answer is in two parts.

Firstly I must repeat the advice I gave you in the introduction and implore you to open yourself up to the subtlety and music of language – a process the previous chapters have hopefully contributed to. As the great business writer John Simmons regularly points out, better writing starts with better listening and reading. The more high quality raw material you expose yourself to, the greater your chances of eloquence. So find some writers whose work you admire and read, read, read. The genre is less important than the quality – anyone from William Shakespeare to Will Self will do, as long as it speaks to you. There is no substitute and no shortcut, but then that shouldn't matter because reading this stuff should be one of life's greatest pleasures.

Secondly I invite you to absorb and implement the seven techniques I'm about to describe. They're practical tools to help you introduce figures in your writing in a way that can yield immediate results. These techniques cut across the descriptions in the previous chapters – instead of saying 'here's a figure and here's how it works', the remainder of this section reverses that approach and says, 'here's a technique that really works, oh and by the way it equates to such and such figure'. They're all highly intuitive – all I'm really doing is calling attention to things you probably do already and presenting them as a toolkit of techniques rather than a series of unconscious approaches. It's more a question of making these unconscious strategies conscious and then using them more often. Once you've internalised the following techniques you'll find yourself using them all the time. Plus they're endlessly flexible, which means you can use them in pretty much any type of writing regardless of subject, audience or objectives. If you want to go deeper, then I heartily recommend *Lend Me Your Ears* by Max Atkinson, a great book on persuasive speaking (rather than writing) that provided some of the examples I've used below.

REPETITION

The first technique I want to highlight is *repetition*. It's something we've seen again and again in this book – multiple instances of a particular word or phrase to underscore a particular point. You can repeat initial words (anaphora) or end and beginning words (anadiplosis). You can create vowel sounds (assonance), consonant sounds (consonance) and – my favourite – stressed syllables (alliteration). The Girl Guides promote themselves with a great alliterative line: 'Dream. Dare. Do'. Staying with dreams and 'd' sounds, Jaguar Cars recently issued the following challenge to US buyers: 'Don't dream it. Drive it'. 'Maybe it's Maybelline', 'If anyone can, Canon can', 'You can be sure of Shell'...the list goes on. If you're stuck for a snappy phrase, try playing around with repetition of some or all of your elements and see where it gets you.

REVERSAL

The next technique to consider is *reversal*. By this I mean a combination of mirror-image elements within a single phrase. Consider this slogan for Bounce fabric softener: 'Stops static before static stops you.' In the first part the noun 'static' is the object of the verb 'stops,' while in the second part the noun 'static' functions as a subject for the verb 'stops.' It's an example of an antimetabole (combined with four alliterative 's' sounds – never be afraid to combine figures for extra impact). The antimetabole is an example of what's called a *syntactic reversal*, a technique that works particularly well with opposing pairs of words. For example, this trim little slogan for a kids shampoo is based on just such a pairing: 'Easy on eyes. Tough on tangles.' As above, alliteration introduces extra melody to the phrase. Job done.

CONTRASTS

Now let's look at *contrasts*. I think we can all agree that, 'To be or not to be' beats, 'Hmm, can't decide if I should commit suicide or not'. In fact the presence of a striking contrast is a consistent feature of effective writing in business, literature, drama and politics and beyond. The main figure of contrasts is *antithesis* – you may recall Neil Armstrong's, 'That's one small step...' from Chapter 4. Other telling examples include:

> *'I stand here before you not as a prophet, but as a humble servant of you, the people.'*
> Nelson Mandela

'It is better to give than to receive'
Acts 20:35

'Two thousand years ago the proudest boast was "civis Romanus sum". Today, in the world of freedom, the proudest boast is 'Ich bin ein Berliner".'
John F. Kennedy

To see how this technique works within the context of business writing, consider the following fictional business waffle:

In this report I want to discuss the need to set clear objectives and create an action plan to address the marketing effort required to take us from sales of under 1,000 units per month to an anticipated figure of 5,000 a month within three years.

If we translate this using the idea of contrasts (particularly taking our cue from Kennedy's example) it could read something like:

This year we've struggled to sell 1,000 units a month. In three years' time we'll have increased that to a remarkable 5,000 units in the same period.

Similarly, contrasts help us translate this:

The points I have described in this email mean we need to do even better in the future.

Into this:

The important thing is not how good we are today, but how much better we can be tomorrow.

As I'm sure you can imagine, you could rework this example by swapping 'how good' for 'how profitable', 'how green', 'how committed' or a million other options and it would still work perfectly.

One final contrasts example. This:

In order to meet our targets, the company must increase investment in all aspects of the business.

Becomes this:

Further investment isn't an option; it's essential for our long-term success.

Clearly we all know what a contrast is, but it's worth looking a little deeper at a number of specific types of contrast that give you ready-made rhetorical tools. The first is *'not this but that'* (Hamlet's 'To be...' line is a good example) or its close alternative *'this but not that'*. The double whammy of negative followed by positive (or vice versa) is a really effective structure and has worked for centuries. Cicero wrote, 'Advice is judged by results, not by intentions', just as a Chairman's Statement in an annual report might say something like, 'Our strategy over the last twelve months should be judged by the results it has achieved, not the controversy it has attracted'. It's a classic one-two attack, and a technique every business writer should know. Which way around should you play it? Well, leading on the negative allows you to end on a positive, which focuses your audience's minds on the affirmative implications of what you're saying. On the other hand, if you want to leave them with an impression of resolute determination then ending on a negative can work a treat: 'You turn if you want to. The lady's not for turning'.

The next contrast I want to mention is *'more this than that'*. It's familiar stuff – 'for better or for worse, for richer or for poorer' or indeed Churchill's chiastic, 'I have taken more out of alcohol than alcohol has taken out of me'. A contrast is an effective way of highlighting a particular point, and can be made to piggyback effortlessly on the many comparative forms that exist within our language – bigger/smaller, better/worse, taller/shorter and so on.

Taking contrasts to extreme we get *opposites*. English is full of opposing pairs (or *antonyms*), in fact they occur in all the major parts of speech – nouns give us truth/lies, happiness/sadness, verbs give us live/die, hurry/wait, adjectives hot/cold or bright/dull, adverbs always/never or quickly/slowly and prepositions up/down, before/after or above/below. With so many opposing pairs to go at it's no surprise that history is liberally peppered with examples:

'Small opportunities are often the beginning of great enterprises'
Demosthenes

'Glory is fleeting but obscurity is forever'
Napoleon

'There is nothing wrong with America that cannot be solved by what is
right with America'
Bill Clinton

A final type of contrast is *phrase reversal*, which is really another way of
referring to the chiasmus we met in Chapter 4 (and a close relation to the
antimetabole's syntactic reversal we saw a moment ago). This gives us
Peter Drucker's, 'Management is doing the right things; Leadership is
doing things right' or Churchill's, 'The optimist sees opportunity in every
danger; the pessimist sees danger in every opportunity.' One word of
advice: try to keep your contrasting clauses – whether you're reversing
phrases, invoking opposites or flagging up contradictions – around the
same length. It makes it easier for the reader to digest and makes sure
nothing stands in the way of the contrast coming through loud and clear.

RHETORICAL QUESTION
I have delighted you long enough with contrasts. The next everyday rhetorical technique I want to suggest is the *rhetorical question*. This builds
on the idea of contrast-as-a-way-of-creating-intrigue we've just seen but
goes further by using an opening statement that actively confuses and
invites the reader to anticipate an answer. It asks them in and makes
them part of the meaning-making process. It gives us such fine lines as,
'Shall I compare thee to a summer's day?' and Churchill's, 'You ask, what
is our policy? I will say: It is to wage war by sea, land and air, with all the
might and with all the strength that God can give us.' Those of us not
required to rouse the nation but just come up with some good business
writing might use rhetorical questions in the form of phrases like: 'That

was the past; what about the future?' or 'So much for the problems; what solutions does our product offer?' Likewise we could translate:

This table explains all the stages in configuring a wireless router.

In to:

So how exactly do you set up a wireless router?

Or:

Having listed last year's major achievements let us know move on to this year's priorities.

In to:

I've described our recent achievements, but what's in the pipeline for next year?

Both of these (and indeed rhetorical questions in general) are examples of excellent linking devices, allowing you to segue seamlessly from one section of an argument to another. It's a very useful, very writer-ly technique. And don't forget that you can chain rhetorical questions together for even more impact. In fact *all* the techniques I describe here can be bundled together in all manner of combinations to excellent effect.

THE GROUP OF THREE

Moving on, the *group of three* (or *rule of three*) is a powerful tool in your persuasive armoury. It speaks of completeness in a way that a two-item couplet can't quite manage (although they certainly have their place), and has a nice rhythm that a four point approach lacks. In fact four points and above is a common-or-garden list – very useful of course but not what we're interested in here. The group of three can work at the word level:

'Location, location, location'

...the phrase level:

'Government of the people, by the people, for the people'

...or the sentence level:

> *'Dogs look up to us. Cats look down on us. Pigs treat us as equals'*
> Churchill

The figure at work here is the *tricolon* we last met in Chapter 4. In his book, *Writing Tools: 50 Essential Strategies for Every Writer*, Roy Peter Clark says, 'Use one for power. Use two for comparison, contrast. Use three for completeness, wholeness, roundness. Use four or more to list, inventory, compile, and expand.' In the world of business writing that might mean something as simple but effective as:

> *This policy will lead to three main outcomes: a new level of commitment from our partners, increased revenue for regional offices, and positive press coverage.*

There's no need for 'firstly', 'secondly' and so on – just punctuate your three points correctly and you'll be golden.

Or we could go slightly further with our tricolon:

> *It's what our staff want, what the market wants, and what society wants.*

> *We need the right people, in the right place, with the right expertise.*

The clever thing about groups of three is that, because your readers implicitly understand the structure, they automatically anticipate its end and feel comfortable with the whole process. Linguists have studied how politicians use groups of three to signal to audiences when they're supposed to applaud. Clearly no one claps business writing (although I'd like them to), but the effect is the same. And our world is saturated with threes – Father, Son, and Holy Spirit, *Sex, Lies, and Videotape,*

Incidentally...

It's often the case that the third clause is the longest ('life, liberty and the pursuit of happiness'). Making the most important item slightly longer than its peers signposts its prestige and means your audience spend that little bit more time reading it. Saving the biggest till last also tends to interfere less with the rhythm of the phrase.

Truth, Justice, and the American Way, Liberté, Égalité, Fraternité. As De La Soul pointed out, three is indeed a magic number. And that's the truth, the whole truth, and nothing but the truth.

INVOLVEMENT

The technique of *involvement* invites the reader to complete the meaning of what they've just read. The message isn't exactly unfinished, but it does encourage the reader's participation. Three sorts of involvement come in useful for business writers. We can deliberately exaggerate a claim that the reader then translates into something more realistic (*hyperbole*), we can intentionally exclude a word or phrase (*ellipsis*), or we can use a part of something to represent the whole (*metonymy/synecdoche*). Suzuki's elliptical slogan, 'Everyday vehicles that aren't', invites us to mentally insert the final, missing 'everyday', while Buick used a metonym in its slogan 'The imports are getting nervous', where 'imports' stood for BMW, Mercedes and so on. The moral of the story is, if you're stuck for a way to grab your reader's attention and draw them into your writing, then try using a figure of involvement to jumpstart the process.

AMBIGUITY

Finally, a rhetorical technique we'll call *ambiguity*. This works by creating a sense of doubt and uncertainty in the reader's mind that you then promptly resolve, either in the text or an accompanying image. The figure of *irony* is a good example. In the US Range Rover promoted their marque with the line 'The British have always driven on the wrong side of the road', accompanied by a suitably dramatic picture of a Range Rover manfully tackling a steep slope off to the side of a road. It only works if the reader knows us crazy Brits do indeed drive on the left (something most potential buyers presumably do understand), and that for a tough car like a Range Rover, the 'wrong' side of the road (in other words, off the road altogether) is in fact the right side.

I've concentrated on headline/slogan/strapline-type writing in this section but these seven rhetorical techniques – repetition, reversal, contrasts, rhetorical questions, groups of three, involvement and ambiguity

– work just as well in body copy, captions, summaries and so on. In fact, *they just work* – that's why the ancients used them and that's why I'm singing their praises today. Figures of speech are timeless and universal – even when the form changes, the intent does not. If this book has a central message it would be something along the lines of, 'Behold the secret life of language! Look at all the marvellous stuff going on under the surface that makes it tick! Imagine what it could do for your writing!' In almost every situation beyond the transmission of pure information the writer who makes an effort to provide his reader with well thought-out words will be rewarded with their attention. The better we write, the more chance we'll be read, which is, surely, the point of the whole wretched activity. Over to you.

BIBLIOGRAPHY, SOURCES AND FURTHER READING

The Guardian Style Guide
Guardian Books, 2007

The Economist Style Guide
Profile Books, 2005

Fowler's Modern English Usage
H.W. Fowler, OUP, 1990

Rewind: Forty Years of Advertising and Design
Various, Phaidon Press, 2004

D&AD Annuals, D&AD, 2000-2009

The Art of Looking Sideways
Alan Fletcher, Phaidon Press, 2001

We, Me, Them and It: How to Write Powerfully for Business
John Simmons, Cyan and Marshall Cavendish, 2006

The Garden of Eloquence: A Rhetorical Bestiary
Willard R. Esp, Harpercollins, 1983

The Garden of Eloquence
Henry Peacham, Scholars Facsimilies & Reprint, 1977

Lend Me Your Ears: All You Need to Know About Making Speeches and Presentations
Max Atkinson, Vermilion, 2004

Metaphors We Live By
G. Lakoff, Chicago University Press, 1981

A Handlist of Rhetorical Terms
Richard Lanham, University of California Press, 1992

Figures of Speech: 60 Ways to Turn a Phrase
Arthur Quinn, Lawrence Erlbaum Associates, 1995

Thank You for Arguing
Jay Heinrichs, Three Rivers Press (CA), 2007

The Oxford English Dictionary
Clarendon Press, 1989

Encyclopaedia Britannica
Encyclopaedia Britannica (UK) Ltd, 2007

The Cambridge Encyclopedia of Language
David Crystal, Cambridge University Press, 1997

Oxymoronica: Paradoxical Wit and Wisdom
Mardy Grothe, Collins, 2008

Never Let A Fool Kiss You
Mardy Grothe, Penguin, 2002

Words as Weapons
Steven Poole, Abacus, 2007

www.wikipedia.org
www.drbilllong.com
www.about.com
www.answers.com
www.figarospeech.com

I've also taken examples of individual figures of speech in use from dozens of books and websites too numerous to mention. I thank you all for your sharp-eyed figure spotting.

INDEX